# Starting with Kant

## STARTING WITH ... SERIES

Continuum's *Starting with...* series offers clear, concise and accessible introductions to the key thinkers in philosophy. The books explore and illuminate the roots of each philosopher's work and ideas, leading readers to a thorough understanding of the key influences and philosophical foundations from which his or her thought developed. Ideal for first-year students starting out in philosophy, the series will serve as an invaluable companion to the study of this fascinating subject.

### AVAILABLE NOW:

*Starting with Berkeley*, Nick Jones
*Starting with Derrida*, Sean Gaston
*Starting with Descartes*, C. G. Prado
*Starting with Hegel*, Craig B. Matarrese
*Starting with Heidegger*, Thomas Greaves
*Starting with Hobbes*, George MacDonald Ross
*Starting with Hume*, Charlotte R. Brown and William Edward Morris
*Starting with Kierkegaard*, Patrick Sheil
*Starting with Leibniz*, Roger Woolhouse
*Starting with Locke*, Greg Forster
*Starting with Merleau-Ponty*, Katherine J. Morris
*Starting with Mill*, John R. Fitzpatrick
*Starting with Nietzsche*, Ullrich Haase
*Starting with Rousseau*, James Delaney
*Starting with Sartre*, Gail Linsenbard
*Starting with Wittgenstein*, Chon Tejedor

# Starting with Kant

*Andrew Ward*

continuum

**Continuum International Publishing Group**

| The Tower Building | 80 Maiden Lane |
| 11 York Road | Suite 704 |
| London | New York |
| SE1 7NX | NY 10038 |

**www.continuumbooks.com**

**British Library Cataloguing-in-Publication Data**
A catalogue record for this book is available from the British Library.

ISBN: HB: 978-1-8470-6184-3
PB: 978-1-8470-6185-0

**Library of Congress Cataloging-in-Publication Data**
Ward, Andrew, 1955-
Starting with Kant / Andrew Ward.
   pages cm. – (Starting with–)
Includes bibliographical references and index.
   ISBN 978-1-84706-185-0 (pbk. : alk. paper) – ISBN 978-1-84706-184-3 (hardcover : alk. paper) – ISBN 978-1-4411-5283-1 (ebook epub : alk. paper) – ISBN 978-1-4411-8419-1 (ebook pdf : alk. paper) 1. Kant, Immanuel, 1724-1804. 2. Philosophy. I. Title.

   B2798.W245 2012
   193–dc23

2011047476

Typeset by Fakenham Prepress Solutions, Fakenham, Norfolk, NR21 8NN
Printed and bound in India

# CONTENTS

# PREFACE

There are – I have found – two striking difficulties in writing an introductory guide to Kant's mature or critical philosophy, his so-called 'Copernican revolution in metaphysics'. The first is his lavish use of technical terminology and the second is his lack of examples at just those points where, to ordinary mortals, they would appear most needed.

In an attempt to ease the problem with technical terminology, I begin with a general introduction to Kant's Copernican revolution in which its overall strategy is first outlined without any use of Kantian terminology. I then try to explain a number of the key technical terms – 'appearance', 'intuition', 'synthetic a priori' etc. – partly by showing how they are designed to operate within my sketch of his revolutionary philosophy. The reader needs to bear this in mind because, in examining Kant's arguments in the two main parts of the book, I assume familiarity with the material in the general introduction, especially with the explanation of technical terms. In other respects, these two parts – Part I dealing with knowledge and metaphysics, and Part II with morality – are virtually self-contained, and it is not necessary to have read both in order to understand either part taken on its own.

As to examples, I have offered them whenever this has seemed helpful. But, above all, I have done so with regard to what is generally agreed to be among the most important – and certainly the most challenging – sections of the *Critique of Pure Reason*, namely, the Transcendental Deduction. I hope that the particular method I have chosen will provide some sense of enlightenment, despite its initial air of paradox. By looking in detail at a *subsequent* section – the Analogies of Experience – I aim to show that the Transcendental Deduction is, in essence, a more generalized instance of the line of argument pursued in the Analogies. Happily, this line of argument is one for which illustrations are readily forthcoming.

Finally an apology: I had planned a short closing section on Kant's aesthetics. But, to my regret, it has taken considerably longer to complete my account of his theory of knowledge, metaphysics and moral philosophy than I had expected. I have, however, outlined the place of aesthetics within Kant's Copernican revolution in the opening section of the general introduction. The bibliography offers a number of general works which expand on this outline.

A. W.

# ABBREVIATIONS AND CONVENTIONS

CJ        *Critique [of the Power] of Judgement* (1790)

**CPractR**    *Critique of Practical Reason* (1788)

G         *Groundwork of the Metaphysics of Morals* (1785)

**Prol**      *Prolegomena to Any Future Metaphysics* (1783)

Quotations from the *Critique of Pure Reason* are referred to by the pagination from the first edition of 1781 (cited as A) and/or the second edition of 1787 (cited as B).

All other quotations from Kant's works are referred to by volume and page number in the German Akademie edition, *Kants gesammelte Schriften*, ed. Deutsche Akademie der Wissenschraften (Berlin: de Gruyter, 1902).

# CHRONOLOGY

Concentrating on Kant's major critical publications together with some other important contemporary philosophical works.

**1710**   Gottfried Leibniz, *Theodicy*
George Berkeley, *A Treatise concerning the Principles of Human Knowledge*

**1720**   Posthumous publication of Gottfried Leibniz's *Monadology*

**1724**   23 April, birth of Immanuel Kant in Konigsberg, East Prussia [now Kaliningrad, Russia]

**1726**   Joseph Butler, *Fifteen Sermons*

**1732–40**   Kant attends (Lutheran) pietist Collegium Fredericianum in Konigsberg

**1739–40**   David Hume, *A Treatise of Human Nature*

**1740–6**   Kant enrolled as a student at the university in Konigsberg, studying mathematics, natural science, philosophy and theology

**1747–54**   Kant employed as a private tutor for various landowning families in the vicinity of Konigsberg

**1748**   David Hume, *An Enquiry concerning Human Understanding*

**1751**   David Hume, *An Enquiry concerning the Principles of Morals*

**1754–6**   Both of Hume's *Enquiries*, along with many of his shorter essays (but not his *Treatise*), published in German translation

**1755**   Kant begins lecturing at the university in Konigsberg

**1757**   German translation of John Locke's *An Essay concerning Human Understanding* (second edition, 1694)

**1765**   Posthumous publication of Gottfried Leibniz's *New Essays on Human Understanding*

**1770**   Kant appointed professor of logic and metaphysics at the university in Konigsberg
Inaugaural Dissertation entitled *On the Form and Principles of the Sensible and the Intelligible Worlds*

**1779**   Posthumous publication of David Hume's *Dialogues concerning Natural Religion* (German translation 1781)

| | |
|---|---|
| **1781** | *Critique of Pure Reason,* first edition [A edition] |
| **1783** | *Prolegomena to any Future Metaphysics* |
| **1785** | *Groundwork of the Metaphysics of Morals* |
| **1786** | *Metaphysical Foundations of Natural Science* |
| **1787** | *Critique of Pure Reason,* second edition [B edition] |
| **1788** | *Critique of Practical Reason* |
| **1790** | *Critique of Judgement* (first edition: minor changes only in later editions) |
| **1793** | *Religion with the Bounds of Reason Alone* |
| **1796** | Kant's last lecture at the university in Konigsberg |
| **1797** | *The Metaphysics of Morals* |
| **1798** | *Anthropology from a Pragmatic Point of View* |
| **1800** | *Logic* |
| **1804** | 12 February, death of Kant in Konigsberg |

# General introduction: Kant's Copernican revolution

I have divided this introduction into four sections. In the first, I offer a very brief overview of Kant's major philosophical claims and their relation to his so-called 'Copernican revolution in metaphysics'. In the second, I outline Kant's distinction between the world of appearances and the world of things in themselves. In the third section, his division of our judgements into three possible types is explained. Whether one likes it or not, there is no hope of grasping the substance of Kant's approach to metaphysical issues without an understanding of this division of judgements. In the final section, an attempt is made to show how, in general, his division of judgements as well as his distinction between appearances and things in themselves relate to his Copernican revolution in metaphysics.

## Kant's major philosophical claims

Kant was struck by the dismal lack of progress in metaphysics, compared with the spectacular advances that had been made in mathematics and natural science. This led him to seek a new approach to solving the problems of metaphysics: an approach that would be along similar lines to the revolutions which, he held, had already made possible the great strides in mathematics (he especially singles out Euclidean geometry) and natural science (by which he essentially means Newtonian physics). Both these disciplines are, he held, in possession of theorems or laws which are everywhere accepted as giving us knowledge of objects that holds necessarily and universally.

As he saw it, the revolutions in mathematics and natural science had arisen as a result of the investigators *themselves* contributing the basic concepts or laws of their respective disciplines (rather than attempting to derive them from experience). For example, in the case of geometry, Kant claims that the mathematician himself provides the basic concepts (*line, triangle, circle*, etc.), and then, with the aid of figures constructed in accordance with these concepts, reaches conclusions that hold with *universality* and *necessity* for all figures of this type. So, for Kant, a typical case of this procedure would be when a mathematician draws a diagram, in accordance with his concept of a *triangle*, and proceeds to demonstrate, on the basis of this single figure, that the internal angles of *all* (plane) triangles *must* add up to 180 degrees. Here, according to Kant, is an example of mathematics providing us with knowledge that holds necessarily and universally, viz. with regard to triangular figures.

But what might an analogous revolution be like in metaphysics? Kant thinks of this science, or presumed science, as divided into two main parts. In the *first* part, metaphysics seeks to investigate the fundamental grounds that enable us to gain knowledge of objects by employing our senses: these objects are what Kant also calls the 'objects of [sense] experience', and they are, in effect, the objects in space and time. So, in its first part, metaphysics is concerned with the *foundations* of our experience of the objects in space and time (nature). In the *second*, and most important, part, metaphysics seeks to learn about those objects or capacities which entirely *transcend* our sense experience: most crucially, metaphysics is concerned here with the possible existence of God, the immortality of the soul and the freedom of the will. Yet, in the case of both parts, Kant always thinks of metaphysics as striving to find truths that can be established *independent of experience* – even if these metaphysical truths may enable us to acquire knowledge that does depend on experience. For instance,

Kant believes that, in its first part, metaphysics can prove, entirely independent of experience, the principle 'Every event must have a cause'. As a result, he thinks that our very capacity to know about any particular event in nature on the basis of experience, e.g. to discover by means of perception that a certain lake is freezing or a particular apple is falling to the ground, necessarily depends, in part, on the truth of this general principle.

In seeking to outline his intended revolution in metaphysics, Kant draws a famous comparison with the revolutionary method inaugurated by Copernicus: 'Failing of satisfactory progress in explaining the movements of the heavenly bodies on the supposition that they all revolved around the spectator, he [Copernicus] tried whether he might have better success if he made the spectator to revolve and the stars to remain at rest. A similar experiment can be tried in metaphysics ...' (B xvi–xvii). In fact, this 'similar experiment' is only meant to apply directly to the attempt by metaphysicians to uncover the *foundations* of our experience of nature (metaphysics in its first part). It is not intended to apply to their attempt to obtain knowledge of those things that entirely *transcend* our sense experience (metaphysics in its second part). Even so, why is Kant drawing a comparison with Copernicus's revolutionary way of looking at the relationship between the earth-bound spectator and that spectator's observed movements of the heavenly bodies?

The main point of his comparison is this. It has traditionally been assumed that the objects in space and time exist and behave entirely independently of our experience (rivers and volcanoes, for instance, are not thought to be dependent for their existence and behaviour on the possibility of our experiencing or perceiving them). But, on this traditional picture, no genuine progress has been made in metaphysics. So, instead of assuming that spatio-temporal objects exist and behave quite independently of our possible experience, let us, at least as an experiment, suppose, on the one hand, that the *sensuous forms* within which the objects of experience can exist, viz. space and time, are contributed by our mind and, on the other, that the fundamental *concepts* and *principles* by means of which the objects of experience (spatio-temporal objects) can behave are also contributed by our mind. On this dual hypothesis, it would certainly seem possible for metaphysics to be put onto the secure path of a science, at least with regard to its first part, viz. the part dealing with the foundations of our knowledge of spatio-temporal objects. For if our mind contributes both the sensuous forms in which these objects can alone exist (space and time) and the fundamental concepts and principles governing their behaviour, then – by examining these features of our mind – we can reasonably hope to explain how, in respect of its overall structure, our experience of spatio-temporal objects is possible. These features would exist *independently* of our experience of spatio-temporal objects (since they must exist in us prior to our having any such experience) and yet they would *make that experience possible*.

In sum, just as Copernicus was enabled to explain the movements of the heavenly bodies by supposing that we, the spectators, make a significant contribution to our experience of these bodies, so Kant believes that he will be enabled to explain the existence and behaviour of spatio-temporal objects, at least in regard to their most fundamental features, by supposing that our mind makes a significant contribution to our experience of these objects.

However, even if such a revolutionary way of considering the relationship between our mind and spatio-temporal objects would enable metaphysics (in its first part) to explain how we could have, independent of any experience, knowledge of these objects, we would not thereby have justified this revolutionary move. The most that would have been shown is that if we *assume* that the objects of experience conform to certain faculties of our mind, metaphysics can then explain how it is possible for us to have the perceptual knowledge of objects that, as Kant holds, we undoubtedly do have. But the success of his Copernican-style revolution, even with regard to metaphysics in its first part, will only be fully assured if it can be shown that the possible objects of our experience *must* conform to faculties of our mind. In the first two major divisions of the *Critique of Pure Reason* – the Transcendental Aesthetic and Transcendental Analytic – this is indeed what Kant sets out to establish. He will argue there that our knowledge of objects in space and/or time can only be explained given his Copernican revolution; and, more particularly, he will argue that all possible objects of our experience, all possible spatio-temporal objects, are provably dependent on our mind supplying the basic framework – the pure intuitions (space and time) and the fundamental concepts and principles – within which these objects can exist and behave. In fact, Kant will contend that with, but only with, his Copernican revolution in place, metaphysics, in its first part, will be able to establish the validity of the laws (or principles) lying at the basis of Newtonian science: principles like 'Substance can be neither created nor destroyed' and 'Every event must have a cause'. As we shall see, the proof of these principles of pure natural science will depend on showing that the principles themselves make our *experience* of spatio-temporal objects possible. Accordingly, no recourse *to* experience can be employed in their proof: on the contrary, the principles must be established entirely *independent* of experience.

We will later be examining the ways in which Kant attempts to secure these ambitious and, on the face of it, highly paradoxical claims. What a paradox, you may think, to claim to establish the fundamental principles of nature *without* consulting experience. However, as Kant himself concedes, his very success in putting the first part of metaphysics onto the secure path of science (the part dealing with the foundations of our experience or perceptual knowledge of nature) appears to have devastating repercussions for its second, and most important, part. This is the part which concerns itself with the possible existence of those objects or capacities that entirely transcend our sense experience (most especially, God, the soul and freedom of the will). For none of these transcendent objects, he admits, is required to make our experience of spatio-temporal objects possible. Yet, as he will argue, it is precisely the capacity of certain concepts and principles to make this experience possible that enables metaphysics to justify them. His cardinal conclusion in the *Critique of Pure Reason*, so far as concerns the possibility of metaphysics, is this. Metaphysics can justify concepts, and the principles containing them, in so far as they can be shown to make our experience of nature (the objects in space and time) possible: where such a proof is available, metaphysics *can* be put onto the secure path of a science. But where no such mode of justification is available – as it is not with regard to our ideas of *God, freedom* and *the soul* – metaphysics *cannot* be put onto the secure path of a science.

On the face of it, this is a disastrous consequence for Kant's intended revolution. Why embrace a revolutionary way of thinking about the objects of our sense experience if this effectively debars metaphysics from answering its own central questions? But, as it turns out, this consequence is no sort of disaster at all. For he will argue that unless we do embrace his revolution, it can be shown that there are pairs of arguments that can legitimately be formulated concerning, among other things, a) the size and age of the whole spatio-temporal world and b) the freedom of the will which are mutually self-contradictory. Only if we abandon the traditional picture of the spatio-temporal world as a world that exists *independently* of our possible consciousness and embrace, instead, Kant's revolutionary view, viz. that this world is *dependent* on us – both in respect of the *forms* in which its objects exist (space and time) and in respect of the fundamental *principles* governing their behaviour (principles like 'Event event must have a cause') – can metaphysics be saved from self-contradiction.

The upshot is that Kant now thinks that we are provided with a further proof – this time, an indirect proof – of his Copernican revolution. For no theory can be correct which leads to self-contradiction. Yet, on the not unreasonable assumption that there are only two possible theories of the relationship between the spatio-temporal world and the observing mind – i) the traditional theory in which this world, in its essential elements, exists independently of our possible consciousness and ii) Kant's revolutionary theory in which it is, in important respects, dependent on our consciousness for its existence – only his own Copernican-style theory is free from self-contradiction. It must, therefore, be the correct account of the relationship between us and the objects of our experience.

Despite Kant's brilliantly orchestrated attempt to put metaphysics, in its first part, onto the secure path of science, as well as his powerful attack on the traditional methods employed by metaphysicians to obtain knowledge about what entirely transcends our experience (metaphysics in its second part), there can, I think, be little doubt that the outcome of the *Critique of Pure Reason*, with regard to metaphysical knowledge, is limited. While metaphysics can explain how our experience of spatio-temporal objects is possible, we must accept that it cannot make any progress in respect of its own central questions. So far as our use of theoretical reason is concerned – which is the sole mode of thinking possible within the domain of metaphysics – we cannot determine whether God exists, the soul is immortal or the will is free.

But although *theoretical* reason is unable to make any progress with the central questions of metaphysics, this leaves open the possibility that our *practical* reason can do so. By 'practical reason', Kant understands that use of our reason by means of which we take ourselves to be able to make practical – and most conspicuously moral – decisions and act upon them. In his moral philosophy, notably in the *Critique of Practical Reason*, Kant claims that the demands of our moral experience prove that, in exercising our pure practical reason, our will is free, and that we can have a rational belief (or 'faith' as he also calls it) in the existence of God and the immortality of the soul. So whereas metaphysics fails to provide answers to its own central questions, he thinks that these questions can be answered – and positively – by our moral experience. Yet, he insists, these answers are only possible in so far as we continue to embrace his Copernican revolution. Unless we accept that the spatio-temporal world is, in regard to its basic framework, dependent on our mind (in just the ways he had argued in the *Critique of Pure Reason*), our conviction of the supreme importance of behaving virtuously and of pursuing the highest good (the union of virtue and happiness) will be wholly unfounded.

Kant's moral philosophy is too often treated as a self-contained structure, requiring little or no understanding of his overall philosophical system (known as his 'critical philosophy'). But the fact is that his moral philosophy is an integral part of his Copernican revolution and, in my view, cannot be adequately defended outside it. Without that revolution, freedom of the will would not only be unprovable but actually impossible – and, hence, morality could make no demands upon us. Moreover, the object of our whole moral life – that we accomplish the highest good – can be shown to require us to have rational grounds for believing in God and the immortality of the soul. No such grounds are available on the traditional picture of our relationship to the spatio-temporal world. As Kant sees it, the very possibility of *moral* experience – and not merely *sense* experience – requires his Copernican revolution.

Given that his moral philosophy is held to provide the answers to the central questions of metaphysics, and his theory of knowledge to those questions of metaphysics which deal with the foundations of our knowledge of nature, it might naturally be thought that there could be no room for aesthetics within his Copernican revolution. But, when he turns – in the *Critique of Judgement* – to consider those judgements that we make concerning the beautiful and the sublime, especially in respect of nature, it transpires that aesthetics too must be placed within this revolution. Only if it is, can these aesthetic judgements be justified, and our consciousness of the beautiful and the sublime be assigned its rightful philosophical significance.

In the first place, he thinks that our judgements of beauty and the sublime can only be justified provided that the spatio-temporal world is dependent upon our mind in just the revolutionary way that he had maintained in the *Critique of Pure Reason*. Unless it is, we shall again find ourselves involved in making mutually self-contradictory claims: here, about the beauties of nature and of art. We would also have to deny that artists are creative and can produce works of genuine beauty. In the second place, he thinks that our judgements of natural beauty, when correctly defended, enable us to form a *bridge* between our scientific knowledge of nature and our moral experience. His investigations into our experience of nature have proved that nature itself must be wholly governed by the universal laws of natural science. His investigations into our moral experience have shown that our will is free from the determinism of nature. Yet, at the same time, it is incumbent upon us, as moral agents, freely to bring about *within* nature the supreme object of morality (the highest good). Can our consciousness of nature, as a thoroughly determined system, and our apparently incompatible consciousness of ourselves as free to achieve the highest good within nature be bridged by something further in our consciousness of the natural world? Kant argues that it can. Our consciousness of natural beauty enables us to make a smooth transition from our undoubted experience of the full-blown determinism of nature to our unshakeable conviction that we are capable of realizing, through freedom, the highest good in nature.

So, according to Kant, it is by means of his Copernican revolution in metaphysics that the three key concepts of philosophy – (scientific) *truth*, *goodness* and *beauty* – are individually made possible. Without that revolution, none of these concepts could be justified; but with it, Kant believes that their objects can exist together in mutual and, in fact, self-sustaining harmony.

## Appearances and things in themselves

Kant's distinction between the world of appearances and the world as it is in itself is central to his Copernican revolution. I have, in fact, already been employing the distinction in outlining his views, but without using the terminology of an 'appearance' and a 'thing in itself'. It is now time to explain this terminology.

In common with most philosophers of the seventeenth and eighteenth centuries – as well as many before and since – Kant takes it that in perception we are never directly or immediately acquainted with the cause of our perceptual consciousness. The data which we are given in perceptual consciousness, and which Kant calls 'representations', are entirely *mind-dependent*. (Descartes and Locke call these data 'ideas' and Hume calls them 'impressions'.)

Now according to a large number of these philosophers, including Descartes and Locke, in any case of genuine perception, the representations are both caused in the mind by objects that exist entirely independently of the observing mind *and* these objects themselves exist in space and time. So, on this theory of perception, often referred to as the 'representative theory of perception', if you perceive a ship going downstream, you would *not* be immediately conscious of this spatial object and its changing state, but only of a manifold of (successively apprehended) representations in your mind. What exists in space and time – here, a ship going downstream – would only be *indirectly* perceived, i.e. via these serial representations which the object has caused in your mind. On this theory, every spatio-temporal object exists entirely *independently* of your acts of perception (which themselves consist of a series of representations of what is occurring in the spatio-temporal world). Kant calls an advocate of the representative theory of perception 'a transcendental realist'. Using Kant's terminology, the object that, on this theory, is indirectly perceived exists as *a thing in itself* in space and time: and this spatio-temporal object (a thing in itself) does not depend in any way on an observer's mind in order to exist as such an object.

Kant rejects the transcendental realist's position in favour of the view that the spatio-temporal object is always an *appearance*. When an observer is conscious of an appearance, that appearance is constituted by the manifold of (successively apprehended) representations which has been produced in the observer's mind; more particularly, it has been produced in what Kant calls 'the faculty of sensibility'. Sensibility is the mind's faculty for receiving representations; and, in our case, Kant holds that it has two forms, inner and outer sensible intuition. When the mind apprehends a manifold of representations, in its faculty of sensibility, the representations are caused by an object (or objects) which exists independently of the mind: this much is common ground between Kant and the transcendental realist. But, for Kant, *this* object – a thing in itself – is *not* what you perceive in space and time (as the transcendental realist claims). What you perceive is an *appearance* (in your faculty of sensibility), which is constituted by the manifold of representations. Space and time are, for Kant, *equated* with the two forms of our sensibility: space with outer sensible intuition and time with inner sensible intuition. An appearance, therefore, is always a mind-dependent phenomenon – it exists only as an actual or possible object of perceptual consciousness (in space and/or time) – and it contrasts with a thing in itself which exists entirely independently of our consciousness (though not, for Kant, in space or time since, for him, both space and time belong *only* to our faculty of sensibility).

So on the Kantian view, known as 'transcendental idealism', the appearance *is* the object of your spatio-temporal experience, and Kant equates space and time with your outer and inner sensible intuitions respectively. When you perceive a spatio-temporal object, you do not perceive it inferentially or indirectly but immediately; and this object, viz. an appearance, is constituted by a manifold of representations which has been caused in your sensibility by a thing in itself or things in themselves. On this theory, you can have no perceptual knowledge *whatever* of any thing in itself. All your perceptual or sensible knowledge is confined to what is apprehended in your forms of sensibility, together with any contribution that the understanding must additionally make in order to be conscious of these representations as a spatio-temporal object or objects.

Kant regards these two theories, transcendental realism and transcendental idealism, as exhaustive of the serious possibilities for explaining how we experience spatio-temporal objects. Both theories accept that there exists a thing in itself or things in themselves as the cause of the manifold of representations that is apprehended in the subject's faculty of sensibility. But whereas the transcendental realist holds that the spatio-temporal object (a thing in itself) is known, and can only be known, *indirectly*, i.e. by means of an *inference* from these apprehended representations to their cause (the object) existing in space and time independently of the subject, the transcendental idealist holds that the spatio-temporal object (an appearance) is *immediately* experienced in the subject's sensibility; and, more particularly, in its forms of outer and inner sensible intuition, which are themselves equated with space and time respectively. For the transcendental idealist, therefore, the whole spatio-temporal world of objects (nature) is merely a world of appearances. Appearances, unlike things in themselves, can have no existence other than as actual or possible objects of perceptual consciousness. They are mind-dependent phenomena. In sum, according to the transcendental idealist, spatio-temporal objects (since they are one and all appearances) can have no existence independently of the possibility of being experienced by us:

> What we have meant to say is that all our intuition is nothing but the representation of appearance; and that the things which we intuit are not in themselves what we intuit them as being ... and that if the subject, or if only the subjective constitution of the senses in general, be removed, the whole constitution and all the relations of objects in space and time, nay space and time themselves, would vanish. As appearances, they cannot exist in themselves, but only in us.
>
> *(A 42/B 59)*

A final point: in giving this brief outline of Kant's basic distinction between appearances and things in themselves, I have obviously not explained Kant's *grounds* for rejecting transcendental realism and accepting his own view, transcendental idealism. His principal grounds will form a major part of our future discussion of the *Critique of Pure Reason* (and he provides additional grounds in some of his later works on morality and aesthetics). But it is important, before we involve ourselves in some of the intricacies of Kant's arguments, to have an appreciation of the overall structure of his own position (transcendental idealism) and how it contrasts with what he takes to be the only serious alternative position (transcendental realism).

# The division of judgements

There are, according to Kant, three possible types of judgement, which he calls: 1. analytic a priori; 2. synthetic a posteriori; and 3. synthetic a priori.

## Analytic a priori judgements

I will explain what Kant understands by an 'analytic judgement' and an 'a priori judgement' before putting the two together. An analytic judgement is a judgement in which the meaning of the predicate term is included in that of the subject term. (Kant confines his explication to subject-predicate judgements, and I shall do the same.) Thus the judgement 'All sisters are female siblings' is an analytic one. For the term 'sister' is equivalent in meaning to 'female sibling'; and, hence, as Kant puts it, the meaning of the predicate term is 'already contained' in the meaning of the subject term. The test of whether a judgement is analytic is the principle of contradiction: if, when the judgement is denied, the result is a self-contradictory judgement, given the meaning of the terms involved, then the original judgement is analytic. Thus the denial of the judgement 'All sisters are female siblings' is 'It is not the case that all sisters are female siblings', which, given the meaning of the terms involved, is self-contradictory.

An a priori judgement is one that holds *independent of experience.* For instance, in order for the judgement 'All sisters are female siblings' to be established, there is no need to consult experience, once the meanings of the terms involved are understood. (Of course, experience may be necessary in order to grasp the meaning of the terms involved in the first place – this is the case with 'All sisters are female siblings' – but *once* the meaning of the individual terms involved is grasped, no recourse to experience is required in order to establish the judgement.)

Although the term 'a priori' means *independent of experience,* Kant says that there are two 'sure criteria' of – two certain means of identifying – an a priori judgement. First, if the judgement claims *necessity,* then it holds, if it holds at all, independent of experience. Take the judgement 'Every event must have a cause'. This judgement claims that it is necessary that an event has a cause, since 'must have' is here equivalent to 'necessarily has'. Second, if the judgement claims to be strictly *universal* in scope (holding for all cases, actual and possible, without exception), then it holds, if it holds at all, independent of experience. In the judgement 'Every event must have a cause', it is being claimed that any event whatever, whether actual or possible, has a cause. The reason why Kant thinks that necessity and strict universality are both sure criteria of the a priori is this. The only possible way to establish that a judgement holds necessarily or with strict universality is independently of experience. No judgement that *depends* on experience in order to be established could claim to hold with necessity or strict universality. For although experience can establish that something *is* the case or *probably is* the case, it can never establish that something is *necessarily* the case or *must be* the case. Hence, only an appeal to what is *in*dependent of experience could ever establish a judgement that carries necessity with it. Similarly, although experience can establish what Kant calls 'comparative universality', it can never establish 'strict universality', i.e. where no exception is allowed as possible. When it was claimed that all swans are white, this was based on an inductive generalization from all experienced cases (to date) of swans. But even at the time that the judgement was believed to be true as a matter of fact, it only claimed *comparative* universality: a counter-example was always allowed to be possible. Experience can never establish strict universality, as in 'Every event must have a cause' (where no exception is allowed as possible). Accordingly, if a judgement claims strict universality, it can only be established, if it can be established at all, independent of experience.

(It has been claimed that there are some judgements that carry necessity with them even though this must be established, or partly established, by appeal to experience. An example would be the judgement that anything that counts as a piece of gold must have an atomic number of 79. I shall not pursue this claim because, although it has been impressively defended, it does not affect the central points that Kant wishes to draw from his concept of the *a priori*.)

It is worth remembering that Kant does not *define* an a priori judgement as one that holds with necessity and/or strict universality. It is defined as a judgement that holds independent of experience. Necessity and strict universality are two sure means of *recognizing* an a priori judgement, a judgement that holds independent of experience. From now on, I will, in general, simply refer to 'universality' as one of the sure criteria of the a priori, as Kant himself normally does. But this will always imply *strict* not comparative universality. When comparative universality is intended, I will make this clear.

So, if we now put our understanding of 'analytic' and 'a priori' together, we can see that an analytic a priori judgement is: a) a judgement where the meaning of the predicate term is included or thought in the meaning of the subject term; and b) a judgement that is established independent of experience. Actually, all analytic judgements must be a priori; since whenever the meaning of a judgement's predicate term is included in its subject term – as with 'All sisters are female' – *no* recourse to experience can be necessary in order to establish the judgement. Hence, it must be a priori.

## Synthetic a posteriori judgements

Again, I will split the explanation into two halves before combining them.

A synthetic judgement is one in which the meaning of the predicate term is *not* included in the meaning of the subject term (confining the explanation to subject-predicate judgements). Accordingly, the denial of a synthetic judgement is not self-contradictory. For example, the judgement 'All men are mortal' is a synthetic one, since *being mortal* is no part of the meaning of the subject term 'man'. Hence, denying the judgement does not result in a self-contradictory one, even though the resultant judgement, 'All men are not mortal', is *factually* false.

An a posteriori judgement is a judgement that *is* dependent on experience in order to be established. Thus the judgement 'Copper dissolves in sulphuric acid' requires experience in order to be established. Note that although the judgement is a general one – since it is claiming that copper always dissolves in sulphuric acid – the judgement only claims *comparative*, not strict, universality: the generalization is based on an inductive generalization from observed cases, and an exception would be admitted as possible.

So a synthetic a posteriori judgement is: a) a judgement in which the meaning of the predicate term is *not* included in the meaning of the subject term; and b) a judgement that *does* require experience in order to be established. Both the judgement 'All men are mortal' and the judgement 'Copper dissolves in sulphuric acid' are, in fact, established synthetic a posteriori judgements. Experience is required to establish them, and experience, together with an inductive generalization, has shown that they are hold, or probably hold, in all cases – although, of course, the universality here claimed is only comparative. Kant, in common with many others, frequently refers to synthetic a posteriori judgements as empirical or factual judgements.

## Synthetic a priori judgements

Since the individual terms 'synthetic' and 'a priori' have already been explained, it can easily be seen that a synthetic a priori judgement is: a) a judgement in which the meaning of the predicate term is *not* included in the meaning of the subject term; and b) a judgement that can only be established, if it can be established at all, *independent of experience*.

The judgement 'Every event must have a cause' is a synthetic a priori one. For given the meaning of 'event and 'cause', the meaning of the predicate term is not included in that of the subject. So the judgement is synthetic. (The judgement 'Every event must have a cause' should not be confused with 'Every effect must have a cause'. The latter judgement is analytic, since the meaning of the term 'effect' includes within it the concept of *having a cause*.) But the judgement 'Every event must have a cause' also claims necessity ('must have') as well as strict universality (the 'every' is taken here to apply to all actual and possible cases of an event). So it must be a priori, since no judgement that claims either necessity or strict universality can be established by appeal to experience.

Even though the notion of a synthetic a priori judgement is not, on Kant's terminology, a self-contradictory one, it is far from clear *how* such a judgement can be established. Whereas an analytic a priori judgement can be established by *analysis* of the meaning of the terms involved (and thereby determining whether the denial of the judgement is self-contradictory), and a synthetic a posteriori judgement can be established by appeal to *experience*, both these routes are barred for a synthetic a priori judgement. Neither an analysis of the terms involved can do the trick (since the judgement is synthetic) nor an appeal to experience (since the judgement, because it claims necessity and universality, holds, if it holds at all, independent of experience). It would be no exaggeration to say that the issue of *how* to establish synthetic a priori judgements is the central one for Kant's whole critical philosophy. I shall try to outline why this is so, at least with respect to metaphysics, in the final section of the introduction.

(Given the meaning that Kant has assigned to the terms 'analytic', 'synthetic', 'a priori' and 'a posteriori', it follows that there can be no room for an analytic a posteriori judgement. For such a judgement, being analytic, must have the meaning of its predicate term included in that of the subject term; and, hence, no dependence on experience could be required in order to establish it.)

\*

Note that, on the definition of the terms 'a posteriori' and 'a priori', it is possible to have a posteriori and a priori concepts as well as judgements. An a posteriori (or empirical) concept is a concept that is acquired either directly or indirectly from experience. The majority of our concepts are, as Kant agrees, of this kind. Thus, the concept *sister* is an a posteriori (or empirical) concept as is the concept *copper*. An a priori concept, on the other hand, is one that is not acquired through experience. As we shall see, Kant believes that there are a number of a priori (or pure) concepts, and these will prove crucial. The concept *cause* is, he holds, an example of a genuine a priori concept; he will argue that our mind, more especially, our understanding is in possession of this concept prior to, and so independent of, our having any experience – and so it is with all genuine a priori or pure concepts.

# Synthetic a priori judgements and the possibility of metaphysics

Kant believes that the success or failure of metaphysics depends on understanding how synthetic a priori judgements can be established (see B 19). Why does he think this?

The answer is that he contends that *all* the judgements of metaphysics are synthetic a priori, whether these judgements are concerned with the foundations of our knowledge of the possible objects of the senses (metaphysics in its first part) or whether they are concerned with questions that entirely transcend sense experience (metaphysics in its second part). Consequently, there seems no reasonable hope of making any progress in metaphysics until we can grasp how, if at all, synthetic a priori judgements can be established.

It is at this point that the revolutions, already achieved, in mathematics and natural science come to have decisive importance. For, Kant claims, all the significant judgements of both these disciplines either are synthetic a priori or contain an essential part which is. (For example, the judgement in pure natural science, 'Every event must have a cause', is a synthetic a priori judgement, on the grounds given in the last section.) Now since – as Kant maintains – it is agreed on all sides that we are already in possession of universal and necessary knowledge provided by these two disciplines, he comes up with the following plan of campaign. Let us first enquire how it is possible for us to know the synthetic a priori judgements of mathematics and pure natural science (which we already possess). Once we have discovered *how* this knowledge is possible in these two disciplines, we should be in an excellent position to see *whether* it is possible for us to know any of the synthetic a priori judgements in metaphysics.

His investigations will lead him to conclude that synthetic a priori judgements about objects are possible in mathematics and natural science because, but only because, the spatio-temporal world is a world of appearances and our mind provides the fundamental concepts governing our experience of this world. Once it has been established that these two disciplines deal with appearances, and not things in themselves, Kant believes that we can explain how the judgements of mathematics and pure natural science – despite being synthetic – *must* apply to *all* the possible objects in space and time (and, hence, are also a priori judgements). The explanation, in the case of both disciplines, is the same: the synthetic a priori judgements of mathematics and pure natural science make it possible for us to experience spatio-temporal objects. For instance, Kant argues that the judgements of Euclidean geometry can be shown to lay down our possible experience of the structural relations of *spatial objects* (thus, any plane triangular object that we could perceive must have its internal angles adding up to 180 degrees). Similarly, he argues that the judgements lying at the basis of natural science can be shown to make possible our experience of the *behaviour* of spatio-temporal objects (thus, any change that we could perceive must have a cause). In order for our apprehension of a manifold of representations to *count* as the experience of any spatio-temporal object(s), this manifold must conform to synthetic a priori judgements of mathematics and pure natural science.

If Kant can make good this explanation of how our experience of nature is alone possible, his Copernican-style revolution – which he first put forward merely as a hypothesis – will have been shown to be correct not only of our possible *experience* of objects but, even more significantly, of the possible *objects* of our experience (the objects in space and time). For if the spatio-temporal world is a world of appearances only, it follows that what holds for our possible experience of spatio-temporal objects must equally apply to those objects themselves. Since appearances – as mind-dependent entities – can only exist in so far as they are capable of being experienced, it follows that any limitations that are placed on our capacity to experience spatio-temporal objects must equally go for the possible existence of these objects.

But why should the truth of Kant's Copernican revolution – in which the objects of our experience must conform to our faculties for experiencing objects – help us in our quest to see if *metaphysics* can be put onto the secure path of a science? The answer is that so far as metaphysics concerns itself with the foundations of our knowledge of the objects of the senses (its first part), metaphysics can now be shown to be a science. For, on Kant's revolutionary position, the synthetic a priori judgements lying at the foundations of natural science – like the judgement 'Every event must have a cause' – can be proved to make our experience possible, and yet they can be established on the basis of theoretical reason alone. They are, therefore, not only judgements *of* metaphysics, but *provable* judgements of metaphysics. On the traditional position, however, viz. transcendental realism, there can be no grounds whatever for believing that these foundational judgements of natural science will be provable: quite the opposite, as Kant will show.

Yet, even on his Copernican-style revolution, the foundational judgements of pure natural science are provable only because they can be shown to make our sense experience possible, viz. our perceptual knowledge of spatio-temporal objects (appearances) possible. Where the judgements of metaphysics have nothing to do with our sense experience – as with all the judgements forming the second, and central, part of metaphysics – they plainly cannot be justified by showing that they make this experience possible. Yet these judgements too are synthetic a priori. Thus the judgement 'The soul is immortal' is a synthetic judgement (since the meaning of 'immortal' is not included in the meaning of 'the soul') as well as an a priori judgement (since it can be established, if it can be established at all, only independent of sense experience). It transpires, therefore, that theoretical reason is quite unable to prove *or* disprove any of the metaphysical judgements that transcend our sense experience. For these synthetic a priori judgements – far from helping to make our sense experience possible – refer to things in themselves, i.e. to objects that exist, if they exist at all, wholly *independently* of any possible sensible intuition. As a result, they are incapable of proof or disproof by theoretical reason since, as Kant will argue, without any data provided by the senses, our theoretical reason is simply unequipped to determine the truth or falsity of any synthetic judgements about objects. Hence, metaphysics, in its second part, *cannot* be put onto the secure path of a science.

It remains to be seen whether our *practical* reason can establish the truth or falsity of those judgements – concerning the existence of God, the immortality of the soul and the freedom of the will – which metaphysics itself has so comprehensively failed to determine.

# PART I

# The Revolution in Metaphysics – *Critique of Pure Reason*

Part I attempts to identify and explain the main claims of the *Critique of Pure Reason*. In the opening chapter, dealing with the Transcendental Aesthetic, we will see why Kant holds that space and time must be equated with our forms of sensible intuition, and why, in turn, this explains how the synthetic a priori judgements of mathematics are possible. The second chapter will take up the major issues that Kant discusses in the Transcendental Analytic. It is here that he offers his explanation of how, in general, there can be synthetic a priori knowledge of objects; and it is here, too, that he provides proofs of the synthetic a priori principles lying at the foundations of natural science. If these proofs are successful – and we will be examining the most important ones – he will have shown that all spatio-temporal objects must obey universal and necessary laws that derive from our own mind. In the final chapter, which considers issues discussed in the Transcendental Dialectic, we will see why Kant rejects the claims of metaphysics to provide us with any knowledge that transcends experience, in particular any knowledge concerning God, freedom or the immortality of the soul.

# 1

# The Transcendental Aesthetic: space, time and mathematics

We saw, in the general introduction, that Kant's plan of campaign is to begin by finding out *how* it is possible for mathematics and pure natural science to provide us with synthetic a priori knowledge of spatio-temporal objects (as, he holds, they undoubtedly do). Once this initial step has been accomplished, he will proceed to see *whether* metaphysics can provide us with any synthetic a priori knowledge of objects. Since our capacity to have any perceptual knowledge of spatio-temporal objects requires that representations are first presented to us in sensibility, Kant starts his investigations into our synthetic a priori knowledge of these objects by examining the relationship between our forms of sensibility (outer and inner sensible intuition), on the one hand, and space and time, on the other. This opening part of the *Critique of Pure Reason* is entitled the 'Transcendental Aesthetic'.

In the course of the Aesthetic, he will argue that space and time must be equated with our forms of outer and inner sensible intuition respectively. He takes it that, at best, there can be only

three plausible views concerning the status of space and time, and
he briefly describes them in the following passage:

> What then are space and time? Are they real existences? Are they
> only determinations or relations of things, yet such as would
> belong to things even if they were not intuited? Or are space
> and time such that they belong only to the form of intuition,
> and therefore to the subjective constitution of the mind, apart
> from which they could not be ascribed to anything whatsoever?
> *(A 23/B 37)*

According to the first view, space and time exist not only independently
of our possible consciousness, but independently of any objects (things
in themselves) in space or time. This is, or at least is taken to be,
the Newtonian or absolute view of space and time; and it is the
view being referred to when it is asked whether space and time are
'real existences'. The second view is that space and time do exist
independent of our possible consciousness (like the first view), but
*not* independently of objects (things in themselves). This is taken to
be the Leibnizian or relational view; and it is what is being referred to
when it is asked whether space and time are only relations of things
[in themselves], yet such as would belong to these things 'even if they
were not intuited'. The third view is that space and time belong only to
our mind's forms of sensibility (outer and inner intuition respectively),
and hence can have no existence independent of our possible sensuous
consciousness. This is Kant's own view; and it is what is being
referred to when it is asked whether space and time belong only to the
subjective constitution of the mind.

Kant presents two different types of argument in favour of
his own view and against the alternatives. First, arguments are
presented that depend on how we think of objects in space and
time, independently of any particular empirical data that these
objects may manifest. These arguments are all listed under what he
calls 'metaphysical' expositions. Second, arguments are presented
that start with the synthetic a priori judgements of mathematics
and, from these judgements, certain key conclusions are drawn
about the status of space and time. These are termed 'transcendental' expositions. (By the time of the Aesthetic, Kant takes it that
we will *acknowledge* that mathematical judgements are synthetic a
priori: he has already argued for this position in the introduction

to the *Critique of Pure Reason*. I will be outlining why he adopts the position later in this chapter.)

Since the arguments concerning space and time are, in general, closely analogous, I will take them together. This should help to illuminate some of Kant's individual arguments because, sometimes, remarks that he makes about time help to clarify his position with regard to space or vice versa.

# Metaphysical expositions of space and time

*(A 22/B 37–A 25/B 40 and A 30/B 46–A 32/B 49)*
In discussing the four arguments of the metaphysical expositions, I will follow the numbering in the B edition, not the A edition.

The first two arguments in the metaphysical expositions of space and time are designed to show that our concepts of *space* and *time* are not acquired a posteriori (through experience), but rather exist in us a priori (independent of experience). These first two arguments are numbered 1 and 2 both with respect to space and time. The second two arguments are designed to show that space and time must be sensible intuitions – that is immediate sensuous presentations – and not *general* concepts. These second two arguments are numbered 3 and 4 with respect to space, but, confusingly, they are numbered 3 and 5 with respect to time.

## Argument 1 for space

If we acquired our concept of *space* a posteriori, this would have to be on the basis of appearances (since even the transcendental realist acknowledges that our only immediate consciousness, in any case of the experience of objects, is of the content of representations given in sensibility). But, argues Kant, we could not possibly have arrived at our notion of space through consciousness of the relations between appearances – relations like *alongside of*, *at a distance from*, and so on – because the very capacity to think of given appearances in these relational ways *presupposes* thinking of them as existing together in space.

In the Transcendental Analytic, Kant will defend this claim further. He will argue that the very ability to apprehend a manifold of representations *as* an outer appearance (or appearances) already requires that this manifold be conceived together in a single spatial continuum (by the application of the a priori concepts of the understanding). No empirical consciousness of any given appearance(s) would be possible without the manifold constituting the appearance(s) being first thought together in space. There could be no question of *starting with* the consciousness of given appearances as 'at a distance from one another' or whatever, and acquiring the notion of space *from* this relational consciousness. There could be no question because only in so far as the representations of the manifold have been conceived together in a single extended (and so spatial) continuum could there be any consciousness of given outer appearances at all, and hence the empirical consciousness of these appearances in any particular relation to one another.

# Argument 1 for time

A parallel argument goes for time. We could have no consciousness of given appearances as *co-existing* or *in succession* without having placed the representations, constituting the particular succession or co-existence, together in time. The very possibility of experiencing any particular change of state or co-existence presupposes that the manifold of representations, constituting the given appearances, has been conceived as existing in time (by application of the a priori concepts of the understanding). Consequently, we could not *derive* our conception of time *from* an empirical consciousness of succession or co-existence among given appearances (and hence a posteriori). Again, this argument does not presuppose the correctness of Kant's own position. For the transcendental realist accepts that our only manner of acquiring our conception of *time* a posteriori is through appearances. The difference between Kant's own position, transcendental idealism, and the transcendental realist's is this. The latter believes that we think of time as attaching to things in themselves, and that this thought is made possible by means of our consciousness of succession and co-existence *among* appearances. Kant, on the other hand, holds that the very possibility of perceiving given appearances as existing in a particular relationship of succession or co-existence requires that the representations, out of which these appearances are constituted, have already been conceived as existing together in time. The consciousness of given appearances existing in a particular succession or coexistence cannot *precede* our conception of time, since this very empirical consciousness itself depends on thinking of the given representations together in a single temporal continuum, i.e. in time.

In sum, neither our notion of *space* nor *time* can be derived from our empirical consciousness because, in both cases, what is alleged to be the required relational consciousness among appearances presupposes that the representations, out of which the appearances are constituted, have already been thought as existing in space and/or time. (When we come to the Transcendental Analytic, we shall consider Kant's detailed grounds for this claim, most conspicuously with regard to time: see especially the discussion of the three Analogies of Experience. However, he defends the claim for both space and time, in a highly condensed form, at B 162–4.)

# Argument 2 for space and time

This argument seeks to prove that both space and time must be given a priori (independent of experience). It is claimed that while space can be thought of as empty of appearances – when we engage in geometrical constructions – no outer appearance can be experienced without thinking of it as in space. Hence, space cannot be dependent on appearances for its existence, but must be a condition for their very existence (and hence must exist prior to, and independent of, experience). Analogously with time: time can be thought of as empty of appearances (when engaging in arithmetical calculations or pure mechanics), but no appearance whatsoever can be thought of except as existing in time. Accordingly, time must be a condition of all appearances, and given a priori, i.e. independent of the consciousness of any appearances.

# Argument 3 for space and time

Here, it is contended that space and time are pure intuitions and not *general* concepts. If *space* were a general concept, it must be possible for it to have multiple instances (as the concept *inhabited planet* can have multiple instances). But space is thought of as *essentially* one continuum. Talk of 'multiple spaces' does not imply that there is more than one space: only that we can talk, and be conscious, of different *parts* of one and the same spatial continuum. Space, therefore, cannot be a general concept; hence, it must be a sensible intuition, that is, an immediate sensuous presentation (the only alternative). Yet it cannot be an *empirical* intuition, as is the sensation of a given colour expanse. For whereas we can experience different patches of red (with no requirement that they must each be part of one and the same all-encompassing red expanse), there can be no question of one subject experiencing different spaces (which may or may not turn out to be parts of one and the same space). Space must be thought of as a single intuition – with the parts of space contained within it – and hence the intuition of space must be a priori. If space were an empirical (or a posteriori) intuition, fabricated from a series of empirical intuitions, there could be no requirement that all these different intuitions are thought of as parts of one and the same single intuition.

Similarly with time: *time* cannot be a general concept, since all the parts of time are thought of as necessarily parts of one and the same temporal continuum and, as Kant puts it, 'the representation that can be given only through a single object is intuition' (A 32/B 47). Only an a priori sensuous presentation – a pure sensible intuition – can provide us with the idea of something that is singular (a continuum) within which all empirical temporal states must be located.

(Later, in the Transcendental Analytic, Kant will seek to account for why – as he claims – we think of space and time as essentially singular intuitions. In the Refutation of [Empirical] Idealism, he argues that each of us can only be conscious of ourselves as a single, temporally continuous subject in so far as there is *one* spatio-temporal continuum in which empirical objects can be intuited.)

## Argument 4 for space and argument 5 for time

We think of space and time as given to us as *unlimited* magni-tudes. But, if space and time were general concepts, they could not be so thought, because although concepts can have an unlimited number of instances falling *under* them, no concept can contain an unlimited number of parts in virtue of which it is *applied*. On the other hand, when we imagine drawing a line in space or following a series of changing positions of a point, we are engaging in an activity in intuition (constructing a line, etc.); and in doing so we can always think of extending these activities *without limit*. It is these intuitive progressions alone that can give us the idea of space and time as limitless in extent (see *Prolegomena* sect. 12). Hence it is by means of intuition, indeed a priori intuition, that we are enabled to think of space and time as given to us as unlimited magnitudes. The intuition is a priori because the mathematical activities here required (constructing a line, etc.) do not have recourse to any *empirical* intuition.

*

Collectively, then, the metaphysical expositions of space and time have contended that both are a priori (or pure) sensible intuitions. That is, they are sensuous presentations belonging to the mind's own faculty of sensibility, and the presentations are *independent of any empirical data* (that is why Kant calls them 'pure' as an alternative to 'a priori' intuitions). More strictly, they are pure intuitions when the mind is engaged in mathematical constructions. When we are conscious of sensing empirical data (as in e.g. perceiving a boat going downstream), the spatial and temporal expanses become *empirical* intuitions. But, even then, space and time are still the *forms* of our intuition: they make possible the structural nature of the empirical data – that the data are always sensed as spatially and/or temporally structured in a single continuum – and these forms reside in the mind (in our faculty of sensibility) a priori.

# Transcendental expositions of space and time

*(B 40–1 and B 48–9)*
Kant regards the transcendental expositions as providing the strongest case for his claim that space and time are a priori (or pure) intuitions. These expositions, he says, serve to make his position on space and time 'completely convincing' (A 46/B 63). However, in order to appreciate their force, we need to understand why Kant maintains that geometry and arithmetic are bodies

of synthetic a priori judgements, with geometrical judgements describing the structure of space and the judgements of arithmetic, as well as pure mechanics, describing the structure of time. I shall concentrate – as Kant does – on geometry.

He takes it as uncontentious that geometry is not only a body of true (and proven) judgements but also that it describes relations of extension and of shape, and, as such, it is concerned with demonstrating the properties of *space*. Moreover, he argues in his introduction that its judgements are synthetic a priori (B 14–17). For example, consider the judgement 'A straight line is the shortest distance between two points'. This judgement is clearly synthetic, Kant argues, because however much one may analyse the concepts of 'straight line' and 'shortest distance', the denial of the judgement will never lead to contradiction (the test of an analytic judgement). And he notes that this is hardly surprising when one realizes that the concept of 'shortest distance' is a *quantitative* concept, while that of 'straight line' is a *qualitative* one. But not only is the judgement synthetic, it must also be a priori. For it claims necessity and universality (two sure criteria of the a priori): it claims that *any* straight line is *necessarily* the shortest distance between two points. The same general strategy can be applied, Kant believes, to all the axioms and theorems of geometry; and, in this way, they can be seen to be, without exception, synthetic a priori judgements (not analytic a priori or synthetic a posteriori).

In short, Kant regards it as certainly correct, and plainly acknowledged as such, that 'geometry is a science that determines the properties of space synthetically, and yet a priori' (B 41). But although he has no doubt about the correctness of this claim, he realizes that we do need to explain *how* this can be possible. In fact, it is easy to miss a move here. There are, as we shall see, two issues. First, there is the issue as to how mathematicians *prove* these synthetic a priori judgements; and second, there is the (consequent) issue as to how these proofs can apply to *space*.

On the first issue, let us continue with the example of the straight line. Since the judgement 'A straight line is the shortest distance between two points', is not analytic, it can only be established by consulting *intuition*: that is by immediate sensuous presentation of a line drawn between two points. For since the subject and predicate are not connected in virtue of the meaning of the terms involved, the connection between them can only be made by intuition. But it is no good consulting *empirical* intuition, e.g. by measuring the lengths of a large number of lines that are experienced as straight, and comparing it with the measurement of many other lines that are not, and then generalizing, by induction, the findings. Such a basis of proof would obviously not allow the mathematician to conclude that it is *necessary* that a straight line between any two points is *always* the shortest distance between them. At best, by this empirical procedure, one could reach an empirical generalization (what Kant calls 'comparative universality'); not a judgement that carries necessity and strict universality. Consequently, the intuition must be one that does not rely on any *empirical* data for its proof. Such an intuition can only be a pure (or a priori) intuition: that is, one that exists in the mind (to be an immediate presentation) *independent* of any experience. A pure intuition is achieved, Kant claims, by the mathematician constructing his a priori concept of *a straight line*, either in imagination (strictly in pure intuition) or e.g. on paper. But in drawing the line on paper, in accordance with his a priori concept, the mathematician leaves out of account any *empirical* features of that particular constructed line, considering it only in so far as it satisfies the conditions of his a priori concept. In this way, Kant maintains that the mathematician is having a pure, not an empirical, intuition (just as if he had constructed the line in imagination). For the intuition is *only* dependent on what the mathematician has himself put into the drawing a priori. When the straight line is thus exhibited in pure intuition, what is observed to hold for the construction of this *particular* line – that it is the shortest distance between two points – can serve for *all* other straight lines actual or possible. But the mathematician is only able to prove this property of a straight line *because* his demonstration (or 'showing') appeals to what is observed or exhibited in pure intuition by means of the construction of his a priori concept or concepts. It is this construction alone that can give the required universality and necessity to his proof of the synthetic judgement, despite being based on a single figure. (There is an excellent discussion of this whole procedure in the Discipline of Pure Reason: see A 712/B 740–A 717/B 745.)

So much for the first issue: Kant's explanation of how the mathematician is enabled to demonstrate synthetic a priori judgements in geometry. This very explanation, however, raises the question as to how geometrical demonstrations can hold for the structure of *space*. This is the second issue which is raised by Kant's position on geometry. The feature that he has identified as vital for the success of geometrical demonstrations is that they are made on the basis of constructions in *a priori* (or *pure*) *intuition* (a property of the mind). But, it might be contended, space and time exist independently of us: they are things in themselves or relations between things in themselves. Certainly, this is the position of the transcendental realist (who holds that space and time, and so spatio-temporal objects, exist independent of the observing mind, whether à la Newton or à la Leibniz). And if this position is correct, it would mean that the results of geometrical demonstrations could *not* be held to apply to space with necessity and universality. After all, if the spatial world exists *in itself*, then, in so far as we can have any sensible consciousness of it at all, this must be indirectly or representationally: that is, by means of an image that the object in space causes, or otherwise occasions, in outer intuition. Equally, on this transcendental realist picture, when the mathematician constructs diagrams, and by means of them demonstrates synthetic a priori geometrical judgements, he is proving them by recourse to outer intuition and not to space. So how could the mathematician know that what holds, by means of his demonstrations, for outer *intuition* must hold for *space*? At best, he could only employ a *probabilistic* inference, and claim that it is likely that what goes for outer intuition will also hold for space. But he could have no right to claim that the results of the demonstrations in outer intuition hold with necessity and universality for space.

In the transcendental exposition of space, Kant counters this consequence of transcendental realism by pointing out that since we *do* know that geometry describes the structure of space synthetically and yet with a priori validity, it follows that space must be *identified with* the form of our outer intuition. This identification is necessary since, as he argued in explaining the method by which the mathematician's proofs proceed, we can only explain how the synthetic a priori judgements of geometry are possible in so far as they are demonstrated in a priori intuition. Accordingly, since the judgements resulting from these demonstrations are agreed to hold for the structure of space (with necessity and universality), it follows that space must be one and the same as pure outer sensible intuition. This identification alone can explain how we can know that the synthetic judgements of geometry hold with a priori validity for the structure of space. Kant illustrates this identification with the example of a geometrical demonstration about triangles:

> If there did not exist in you a power of a priori intuition; and if that subjective condition were not also at the same time, as regards its form, the universal a priori condition under which alone the object of this outer intuition is itself possible; if the object (the triangle) were something in itself, apart from any relation to you, the subject, how could you say that what necessarily exists in you as the subjective conditions for the construction of a triangle, must of necessity belong to the triangle itself? ... If, therefore, space (and the same is true of time) were not merely a form of your intuition, containing conditions a priori, under which alone things can be outer objects to you, and without which subjective condition outer objects are in themselves nothing, you could not in regard to outer objects determine anything in an a priori and synthetic manner.
>
> *(A 48–B 65/66)*

An analogous argument is offered with regard to the synthetic a priori judgements of arithmetic and pure mechanics. Only if time is equated with the form of our inner intuition can we explain how these judgements hold for time with necessity and universality.

# Review

Let us review what Kant believes that he has established by the end of the Transcendental Aesthetic. He believes that his metaphysical and transcendental expositions have proved that space and time are one and the same as our outer and inner pure intuitions respectively. Not only does this provide an explanation of how the synthetic a priori judgements of pure mathematics are able to determine the structure of space and time, it will also – and crucially – help him to explain how these same judgements can hold for the *objects* that can possibly be experienced in space and time. Remember that he is seeking an explanation of how mathematics and natural science have been able to provide us with synthetic a priori knowledge of what can exist in space and time, viz. empirical objects. So far as concerns mathematics, he is nearly there but not quite. He still needs to show why the objects that can be experienced *in* space and time must obey the synthetic a priori judgements of mathematics. However, there is one highly significant consequence that can already be drawn from his arguments. Granted that space and time are merely properties of our mind (since they are identified with the form of our outer and inner intuition respectively), it must follow that all the objects of our possible experience, the empirical objects that can exist in space and time, are *appearances* and not things in themselves. Spatio-temporal objects – appearances – must, therefore, be constituted from the manifold of representations (mind-dependent phenomena) that we apprehend in outer and inner intuition.

Before we leave the Transcendental Aesthetic, there is a very general point that is worth noting because it bears on the overall success or failure of Kant's Copernican project. If space and time belong to the subjective constitution of the mind (as Kant maintains), it is not possible for space and time *also* to exist as things in themselves or to be identified with relations between things in themselves. What are inherent properties or modes of a mind cannot be conceived to exist *in their own right* – since they require a substance in which to inhere – and, consequently, they also cannot be conceived to be *relations between* what exists in their own right (since what is an inherent property of a substance cannot be conceived as a relation between substances). This point is important for Kant's moral philosophy because, in order to defend freedom of the will, he needs to maintain that space and time belong *only* to the subjective constitution of the mind, and cannot exist in themselves or as relations between what exist in themselves. Incidentally, he is frequently criticized for overlooking the possibility that space and time might so exist *as well as* existing as pure intuitions. This criticism is unfounded, assuming the validity of his metaphysical and/or transcendental expositions.

# 2

# The Transcendental Analytic: our experience of nature

In the Transcendental Analytic, Kant investigates the role of the understanding in making experience, or knowledge of objects by means of the senses, possible. The understanding is conceived as that faculty of the mind by which we are able to think about or judge any data that is presented to us.

We have already seen, from the Transcendental Aesthetic, that it is by means of our faculty of sensibility that we become conscious of sensuous data (representations), and that its two forms – outer and inner intuition – are equated with space and time respectively. The question now before us is about the contribution that the capacity to *think about* this data makes to the possibility of experience. It is here, in the Analytic, that Kant sets out to explain how the synthetic a priori judgements of pure natural science are possible: that is, how we can be in possession of the fundamental laws of natural science even though these laws can be established neither by experience nor in virtue of the meanings of the terms involved.

In the course of his complex discussion, he will argue that the objects in space and time cannot be in chaos: on the contrary, they must all be governed by, and continue to be governed by unchanging causal laws. As Kant was well aware, David Hume's scepticism about causation had apparently shown that there is no rational ground for supposing that spatio-temporal objects must be in thoroughgoing causal connection; and, even granting that these objects have, up to now, behaved with perfect regularity as a matter of fact, there is no rational ground for believing that they will continue to do so in the future. Hume's causal scepticism was first set out in *A Treatise of Human Nature* (Book I, Part III); but Kant almost certainly knew about it principally from the later *An Enquiry concerning Human Understanding* (Sections 4–7). According to his own account, it was Hume's scepticism about causation that awoke him from his 'dogmatic slumbers', and set him on the path that led to his Copernican revolution in metaphysics.

Near the end of the Analytic – in the Refutation of [Problematic] Idealism – Kant will also argue against the possibility of thinking of oneself as a continuously existing subject while casting doubt on the very existence of spatial objects. A classic version of this form of scepticism about external objects had been maintained by René Descartes in his *Meditations* (1641).

*

Although the Transcendental Analytic is divided into two main divisions, the Analytic of Concepts and the Analytic of Principles, his explanation of how synthetic a priori judgements are possible in pure natural science proceeds by *three* stages:

In stage one, Kant attempts to show that the understanding itself possesses, independent of experience (and so entirely a priori), all the basic concepts by which we are able to think of any manifold of representations, constituting an object of the senses, as falling under any laws. In other words, in so far as we can connect or synthesize such a manifold of representations, given in any form of sensible intuition, under any universal and necessary rules (laws), these laws will invariably employ a priori concepts of our understanding. Thus, Kant will argue that one of the fundamental laws that we seek to apply to the manifold of spatio-temporal representations is the principle 'Every event must have a cause'. This fundamental law employs the concept of *cause*; and this concept, Kant claims, exists a priori in our understanding. These a priori concepts of the understanding he calls 'the categories' or 'the pure concepts of the understanding'.

The task of showing that the understanding possesses, independent of experience (a priori), all the basic concepts, the categories, by which any manifold of representations, constituting an object of the senses, can be conceived as falling under any laws is undertaken in the **Metaphysical Deduction.**

In stage two, Kant attempts to prove that any manifold of representations must obey the categories in so far as it can provide us with any experience, with any knowledge of objects by means of the senses. This stage is more adventuresome than the first. It is one thing to show that *if* we are capable of bringing a manifold of representations, given in any form of sensible intuition, under any laws, the basic unifying concepts employed in the laws must reside a priori in our understanding. It is a further step to show that such a manifold *must* conform to these concepts (and the corresponding laws) in so far as we can have any perceptual knowledge of objects by means of that manifold. After all, the various manifolds of representations, constituting the appearances (the empirical objects of sensible intuition), are given to sensibility *independently* of any action of the understanding. The original apprehension of these representations depends not on the understanding but on the action of a thing in itself (or things in themselves) on our faculty of sensibility. Why, therefore, should appearances obey any of the universal and necessary rules (employing the categories) that depend on the understanding? For instance, in respect of objects existing in *our* forms of sensible intuition, space and time, it would, on the face of it, seem quite possible to experience spatio-temporal objects, even though these objects could *not* be thought of as falling under any laws arising a priori from the understanding. Take the case of an object changing its state: it would certainly *seem* that we could be conscious of witnessing such a temporal occurrence although we could not bring the change of state under any universal rule. Why, for example, should it be impossible to experience water sometimes freezing at 0 degrees centigrade and sometimes not doing so (with the surrounding circumstances the same in every case)?

In fact, Kant will argue that the apparent possibility that experience could be of objects which fail to obey any laws, and, more particularly, laws that employ the categories, is not, in reality, a genuine possibility. He will argue, further, that all the possible *objects* in any sensible intuition whatever must obey the categories (and not merely that all objects that can be *experienced* in any sensible intuition must obey the categories). These tasks are undertaken in the **Transcendental Deduction**.

In stage three, Kant claims that when the categories are applied to our particular forms of sensible intuition, space and time, they yield all the fundamental laws (or principles) by means of which the understanding can think of any objects in space and/or time; and he seeks to show, in detail, how all the possible objects in space and time must, in their various ways, be subject to these principles. For if the objects of any sensible intuition whatever must conform to the categories (as Kant claims to have shown in stage two), then what he calls 'the principles of pure understanding' – which specify how these categories apply a priori to our (spatio-temporal) intuition – must lay down the basic universal and necessary rules for how objects can exist and behave in space and/or time. More specifically, it is here that he will seek to prove that the synthetic a priori judgements of mathematics must hold not only for the structure of space and time, but for all objects that can exist in space and/or time. It is this proof that finally explains how mathematics can yield synthetic a priori knowledge of empirical objects or how – as he sometimes puts it – mathematics can have 'objective validity'. It is also in this third stage that Kant attempts to prove that the fundamental dynamical laws of pure natural science must govern the behaviour of all spatio-temporal objects. The particular subsection devoted to this task, known as the Analogies of Experience, is an especially renowned part of the *Critique of Pure Reason* because it is here that Kant makes his response to Hume's scepticism about causation.

The task of proving both that when the categories are applied to our forms of sensible intuition – spatio-temporal intuition – they yield the fundamental laws, the principles, governing the behaviour of all possible spatio-temporal objects and that mathematics provides the universal and necessary rules governing the possible form or structure of these objects is undertaken in the **Principles of Pure Understanding**.

# The Metaphysical Deduction

*(A 66/B 92–A 83/B 116: the title itself is given at B 159)*
At the time that Kant was writing, there was widespread agreement that Aristotle had exhaustively enumerated all the possible ways or forms in which we can think about any data whatsoever. These 'forms of thought' Kant lists in his Table of Judgements. This table does not, of course, say anything about the content of thought – *what* we can think about – only about the possible ways in which we can put data together into a comprehensible form, that is, into a thought.

He also claims that these judgement forms are a priori: that is, they reside in our understanding independent of our having any experience at all. Presumably the idea is that in order for us to start thinking about any data, the mind must already possess fundamental modes of thought. It might be suggested that at least the *discovery* of these judgement forms must be an empirical matter, since Aristotle will have had to observe how we manage to think about data, including empirical data, in order to enumerate the judgement forms. But I am confident that Kant would not accept that the procedure by which Aristotle formulated the table of judgements counts as an *empirical* one (any more than he would accept that the procedure by which mathematicians demonstrate geometrical theorems by means of construction counts as an empirical one). For Aristotle will not have been concerned with the *content* of any of the judgements, only with their *form*; and for Kant, the capacity to identify form is entirely the province of our understanding or reason. Accordingly, no empirical data (which comprise the content of judgements) have to be taken into account in order to enumerate any part of the Table of Judgements. Hence, the process of its formulation cannot be an empirical undertaking. This is not to say that Kant holds that we can be certain, beyond any possibility of doubt, that we have enumerated the full range of our forms of judgement. It is logically possible that we have failed to identify some of the understanding's modes of thought. But he contends that this possibility is exceedingly slight, given: a) that Aristotle first formulated his table of judgements two thousand years ago and there have been no important changes since that time; and

b) we are seeking within one of *own* faculties, the understanding, for these forms of thought, and these possessions of the mind are not likely to be voluminous. As he says about b):

> [W]hat here constitutes our subject-matter is not the nature of things, which is inexhaustible, but the understanding which passes judgment upon the nature of things; and this under-standing, again, only in respect of its a priori knowledge. These a priori possessions of the understanding, since they have not to be sought for without, cannot remain hidden from us, and in all probability are sufficiently small in extent to allow of our apprehending them in their completeness.
>
> *(A 13/B 26)*

As Kant sees it, then, the mind possesses, independent of any experience, certain judgement forms by which it is alone enabled to think about (or judge) any data; and these forms have been, in all probability, exhaustively enumerated by Aristotle. At the same time, our knowledge of them can give us no information whatever about the content of experience. The forms are listed by Kant under the Table of Judgements (A 70/B 95):

### Table of Judgements

I
*Quantity*
Universal
Particular
Singular

II
*Quality*
Affirmative
Negative
Infinite

III
*Relation*
Categorical
Hypothetical
Disjunctive

IV
*Modality*
Problematic
Assertoric
Apodictic

As I remarked earlier, it is in the Transcendental Analytic that Kant considers not only how the understanding can think about sensible representations, but what role these acts of thought can contribute to our perceptual knowledge of objects. His opening claim – the central claim of the Metaphysical Deduction – is that the concepts that express the most basic ways in which we can think of any objects of the senses as falling under laws must be derivable from the judgement forms. In a general way, this claim is not implausible. For, in the first place, laws concerning objects are, of course, always expressed in *judgements*; and since we are dealing with laws, these judgements will hold *universally* and *necessarily* (as with: '*Whenever* there is a change of state, the quantity of substance *must* remain the same'). In the second place, Kant takes it that, independent of experience, we possess all the fundamental ways in which we *can* connect together any data whatever in a judgement. As I have already noted, these ways are given by the judgement forms listed in the Table of Judgements. Granting these assumptions, it is not unreasonable to hold that any comprehensible laws governing the objects of the senses must, in their structure, derive from the judgement forms (when these are taken to hold universally and necessarily).

Now consider a familiar concept that we use to express a lawful connection between items in the spatio-temporal world, viz. the concept of *cause*. When we think of an object's change of state as happening in accordance with this concept, we are claiming that whenever certain circumstances obtain, that change of state must occur (as in: 'Whenever water in the liquid state is heated to 100 degrees C, under normal pressure, it must change to steam'). In other words, in thinking of an object's change of state as falling under the concept of *cause*, we are thinking of a connection between the object and its surrounding circumstances which, in respect of its structure, instantiates the rule expressed by the hypothetical judgement form (when this carries universality and necessity): If (or whenever) A then necessarily B. In short, when – in our particular forms of sensible intuition, space and time – we think of an object's change of state as falling under the concept of *cause*, we are conceiving of a lawful connection between the changing states which has a parallel structure to thinking of any data whatever as subject to the rule expressed by the hypothetical judgement form (given this carries universality and necessity). Quite generally – granting that the only available ways in which we can think about any data whatsoever are provided by the judgement forms – any laws that we can possibly understand as applying to objects of sensible intuition must derive their *structure* from one or more of these judgement forms, when they express a universal and necessary connection. And the pure concepts of the understanding (the categories), once their use is restricted to a particular form (or forms) of sensible intuition, will exhaustively specify the fundamental ways in which we can think of the objects of this sensible intuition as subject to necessary and universal rules (laws). (Kant makes a stab at explaining the derivation of the categories from the judgement forms – concentrating on the category of *cause* – in Part II, Sections 20–2 and 29, of the *Prolegomena*.)

The categories, then, are not only concepts that reside in the understanding, independent of anything presented to us in sensibility, they are also the sole means by which we can think of a manifold of sensible intuition, and so any appearance constituted by that manifold, as falling under any law(s) and, thereby, as forming a determinate collection or unity. (Thus when the successive representations of water in the liquid state and in the gaseous state are connected by means of the concept of *cause*, they are conceived as *having* to occur in that order in the given circumstances.) Kant deduces the categories from the judgement forms, when these forms are thought of as referring, with necessity and universality, to what is given in sensible intuition. The full list of categories is shown in the Table of Categories or Pure Concepts of the Understanding (A 80/B 106: see p.43 below, where I have followed the slightly simplified table given in the *Prolegomena*, Second Part, Section 21).

Each category is supposed to correspond to the similarly placed judgement form in the Table of Judgements (when the judgement form carries necessity and universality). Thus, as I have attempted to illustrate above, the hypothetical judgement form (under heading III of the Table of Judgements) corresponds and leads to the category of *cause* (under heading III of the Table of Categories). Although it is not clear to me how, in detail, each of these derivations is supposed to go through, Kant's general line of argument does seem clear enough. Granted that the understanding possesses, a priori, all the fundamental ways of thinking about any data whatever – the judgement forms – there will be a corresponding list of categories of the understanding: this list will exhaustively enumerate the fundamental concepts that we can employ for combining a manifold, given in any sensible form of intuition, under laws and so of unifying the representations of that manifold.

Table of Categories or Pure Concepts of the Understanding

I
*Quantity*
Unity
Plurality
Totality

II
*Quality*
Reality
Negation
Limitation

III
*Relation*
Substance
Cause
Community

IV
*Modality*
Possibility
Existence
Necessity

\*

There are two points to bear especially in mind about the Metaphysical Deduction. First, the categories, as they have been deduced from the judgement forms, are, as I have said, the understanding's exhaustive set of concepts by means of which we can think of any manifold of sensible intuition as falling under laws. As such, they tell us nothing about the particular *type* of sensible intuition to which they are to be applied. *Our* sensible intuitions are spatial and temporal; but this feature of our experience has not figured in the deduction of the categories from the judgement forms. As they stand, the categories are the most general rules by which the understanding can alone unify the serial representations of a manifold given in *any* form of sensible intuition. How exactly these categories are to be applied to our – spatio-temporal – sensible intuition has not so far been explained by Kant. It is true that in trying to outline the Metaphysical Deduction, I have illustrated how the category of *cause* would apply in *our* forms of sensible intuition, space and time. I gave the example of a quantity of water (something spatial) changing from the liquid state to the gaseous state (a temporal occurrence). But the grounds for holding that the categories are an exhaustive list of the concepts by which we can think of any manifold of sensible intuition as falling under laws, and so as unified in that form of sensible intuition, has *not* depended on specifying that the manifold is presented in our forms of sensible intuition. It is only in the later Analytic of Principles that Kant will set out how, in particular, the categories apply to spatio-temporal intuition.

Second, you may have the uneasy feeling that, in the Metaphysical Deduction, Kant has performed the philosophical equivalent of conjuring a rabbit out of an empty hat. He must have done so, you may think, on the grounds that, in this Deduction, he is claiming to have shown that the objects that exist in sensible intuition (appearances) must obey the universal and necessary rules which exist a priori in our understanding. Such a claim, you may feel, is obviously preposterous because the understanding has no control over how the manifold constituting objects is given to us in sensible intuition. Accordingly, there can be absolutely no guarantee that the categories will be able to *apply* to objects, i.e. there can be absolutely no guarantee that we shall be able to think of any of the objects of sensible intuition as *conforming* to the pure concepts in our understanding. Hence, even allowing that Kant is right to claim that we possess, a priori, an exhaustive list of the fundamental concepts (the categories) by which the objects of sensible intuition can be grasped by us as falling under laws, and even allowing that he has correctly enumerated what these categories are, he has given no grounds whatever for supposing that we will ever be able to *use* any of the categories in our experience. For it is surely possible that the objects of sensible intuition might be in such chaos, or suddenly become so chaotic, as not to allow us to *employ* the categories; and, yet, objects would still be presented in sensible intuition (for us: in space and/or time).

But such a suspicion of sleight of hand would be misplaced. The argument of the Metaphysical Deduction is *not* that the objects of experience, the objects in sensible intuition (appearances), must conform to the categories. It is only that in so far as we are *able* to think of the objects of sensible intuition as falling under laws, these laws must employ the categories, that is, concepts that are in us (in the understanding) prior to, and so independent of, experience.

Admittedly, this argument, if successful, does show that we cannot have derived concepts like *substance* or *cause* from experience, as the empiricists – and Hume in particular – had claimed. Nevertheless, for all that has been argued in the Metaphysical Deduction, it would indeed seem possible that the objects of sensible intuition should be in such chaos, or suddenly descend into such chaos, that we would find ourselves unable to connect the manifold out of which they are constituted under any universal and necessary rules employing the categories; and, in such an eventuality, it would still seem that objects would be experienced, even though we could not bring their behaviour under any laws at all.

Kant is plainly aware that the Metaphysical Deduction has not shown that the categories must apply to the objects of sensible intuition. Thus, in the introduction to the Transcendental Deduction (which immediately follows the Metaphysical Deduction), he says this:

> Appearances [for all that has so far been established] might very well be so constituted that the understanding might not find them to be in accordance with its unity. Everything might be in such confusion that, for instance, in the series of appearances nothing presented itself which might ... answer to the concept of cause and effect. This concept would then be altogether empty, null, and meaningless. But since intuition stands in no need whatsoever of the functions of thought [the categories], appearances would none the less present objects to our intuition.
> *(A 90–1/B 123)*

I conclude that the Metaphysical Deduction has not attempted the philosophical equivalent of conjuring a rabbit out of an empty hat. This Deduction has not attempted to prove that the categories must apply to all the objects of possible experience from the mere fact that we possess, a priori, the most fundamental concepts – the categories – by which we can think of objects of sensible intuition as governed by laws. Nonetheless, Kant undoubtedly does maintain that all the objects of experience must conform to the categories. In the light of the problems raised in the previous three paragraphs, you may well wonder how he can possibly justify such a claim. It is the burden of the Transcendental Deduction, not the Metaphysical Deduction, to perform this task – a task that Kant himself says cost him more effort that any other part of the *Critique of Pure Reason*.

# Introduction to the Transcendental Deduction and the Principles of Pure Understanding

We have seen from the Metaphysical Deduction that the categories are the mind's basic concepts for enabling us to think of the objects of sensible intuition, appearances, as falling under laws. Although Kant does claim, in this Deduction, that the application of categories is necessary for any *knowledge* of objects, qua appearances, no argument is there offered; and, as we have just noted, he himself acknowledges that it is not obviously correct. For the manifold of representations – and so any manifold capable of constituting an appearance – can certainly be given to us, in sensibility, *independently* of the categories; and if that is so, it would seem to follow that whether or not appearances conform to the categories, the objects of sensible intuition would still exist and be experienced by us (since empirical objects of sensible intuition are all appearances). What alone the Metaphysical Deduction can plausibly be seen as demonstrating is that, in so far as we can have any knowledge of objects of the senses as governed by laws, categories must always play the basic unifying role in these laws.

However, in the Transcendental Deduction, it is argued that categories *must* be applicable to any manifold of representations (whatever the form(s) of sensible intuition in which it is given) if any experience, any knowledge of empirical objects, is to be possible on the basis of that manifold. There can, I think, be no doubt that one of the greatest obstacles to grasping the argument of the Transcendental Deduction arises from the fact that it is largely carried out at an extremely abstract level. One reason for this is that Kant is here attempting to prove that the categories make experience possible *whatever* the form(s) of intuition in which objects are sensed (or, at least, by the time of the B-edition deduction, this is explicitly Kant's claim: see e.g. B 148). From the side of sensibility, all that his proof needs to take for granted is, first, that the objects of experience are to be identified with the objects of sensible intuition – and, hence, can only be appearances and not things in themselves – and second, that what the mind originally apprehends by means of its form(s) of sensible intuition is a manifold of (separately given) representations. He is trying to prove that, in order to grasp any such manifold as an object of experience, the mind must be able to think of the manifold as conforming to categories. Now, plainly, it is very difficult to make out a convincing case for this highly general claim without showing how categories make possible the perception of an object in the only way that *we* can experience objects, viz. as spatial and/or temporal entities. But although Kant does, occasionally, illustrate his argument by showing how it applies to our (spatio-temporal) experience, he largely sweeps on at the very general, and abstract, level. It is only in the later Principles of Pure Understanding that he attempts to show in detail how any of the categories make our own experience possible. One of the problems that this approach has generated is that it has seemed to many commentators that the arguments in the Principles are altogether *different* from the argument of the Transcendental Deduction or, at any rate, very obscurely related to that latter argument.

Fortunately, I believe that the central set of arguments in the Principles of Pure Understanding does help us substantially to understand the Transcendental Deduction, despite the apparent disparity between the two. So my strategy is this. I will first merely summarize the main outlines of the Transcendental Deduction. I will then explain in some detail why, in the Principles of Pure Understanding, Kant believes that the categories – or, more strictly, three of the most important categories – make our own, spatio-temporal, experience possible. I will then attempt to show how Kant's central argument in the Principles of Pure Understanding does illuminate the much more abstract Transcendental Deduction.

# The Transcendental Deduction (in outline)

*(A 84/B 116–A 130/B 169)*
Throughout the Analytic, it is taken for granted that we have no original consciousness of ourselves as existing throughout any given manifold (or series) of representations. Prior to a certain action of the understanding on the manifold, Kant maintains that there is only a series of *disparately* given representations, each accompanied with an *individual* act of self-consciousness or 'I

think'; there is no immediate consciousness of all the disparately given representations of any manifold as occurring to one subject, ourselves. The claim that each of us is not, prior to a connecting action of the understanding or imagination, conscious of being a single subject or I to which all the representations of a manifold present themselves is a crucial one (it is a claim which Kant shares with Hume), and it needs to be remembered for the remainder of the Analytic. It is especially prominent in the Transcendental Deduction, as we are about to find.

The central argument of the Deduction begins with the following observation. If there is to be the knowledge of all the (disparately given) representations of a manifold, these representations need to be brought to what Kant calls 'the unity of apperception': in other words, it must be possible for *one* subject to be aware of *all* the representations of that manifold. For if, for any manifold of representations, a subject of consciousness, an 'I think', merely apprehends a single representation of that manifold, this could only give rise to a series of *separate* acts of self-consciousness (e.g. 'I am aware of A. I am aware of B. I am aware of C.') and could not give rise to the recognition that *one* subject possesses the consciousness of the *whole* manifold ('I am aware of three items, A and B and C.'). How can this unitary consciousness be achieved?

Kant's answer is that only in so far as it is possible to think of the separately given representations of the manifold as *falling under a concept* can there be one subject who is conscious of all the representations of that manifold. For concepts are the means by which we can *combine* a manifold, thereby enabling us to think of the representations of a manifold as forming a unity, as constituting a single unit: concepts bring together, in one thought, in one act of consciousness, the separately given representations, by specifying a determinate relation holding between them. (Thus, the concept of *a triangle* specifies the way in which three lines can alone be thought as forming one spatial area.) It is only because the disparately given representations of a manifold can be recognized as falling under a concept that it is possible for the whole manifold to be present in one act of consciousness. And it is this capacity to bring together a whole manifold in one act of consciousness – through the application of a concept to the manifold, thereby combining its representations in one thought – that makes possible the unity of apperception, i.e. the awareness of that whole manifold by one subject.

We have already seen, from the Metaphysical Deduction, that the mind's fundamental ways of unifying a manifold of representations, given in any form of sensible intuition, are the categories. Hence, the categories are the mind's most basic concepts for recognizing a manifold of sensible intuition in one act of consciousness. In so far, therefore, as there can be the consciousness of an appearance (and every appearance is constituted by a *manifold* of representations given in some form of sensible intuition), the manifold, constituting the appearance, must be capable of being thought by means of the categories.

Now an *object* of the senses is always thought of as capable of determining a subject's apprehension in a given way. For an object of the senses is conceived to exist *distinct* from apprehension; and so the way a subject apprehends it must depend on how the object *itself* is disposed, i.e. on how the manifold constituting it is itself arranged. (For example, if, in normal circumstances, a subject perceives that water is freezing, the subject must apprehend water in the liquid state *followed by* water in the solid state: if a subject is to experience an object, *how* the subject apprehends the manifold constituting the given object – here, water freezing – is dependent on how the object itself is disposed.) Since an appearance, in order to be known, must conform to the categories (and so be arranged in a determinate way), it follows that in apprehending a manifold as an appearance, a subject must also be capable of recognizing that its *apprehension* of that appearance is itself determined in a given way. Consequently, a subject's very capacity to be conscious of an appearance makes possible its consciousness of that appearance *as* an object of the senses.

Moreover, appearances alone can be experienced as objects of the senses. For every manifold of sensible intuition that conforms to the categories and, as such, conforms to determinate rules, is capable of being recognized as an appearance (since an appearance is any manifold of representations, given in some form of sensible intuition, that can be recognized as unified – and, hence, as conforming to categories). But if a manifold of sensible intuition does not conform to the categories, it cannot be recognized as unified (and thus as arranged in a determinate way). Hence, it cannot be conceived as determining our apprehension. Appearances alone, therefore, can be conceived as determining our apprehension of a manifold of sensible intuition; and so they alone can be experienced as objects of the senses. Since appearances, and so the objects of the senses, cannot exist *unless* they are capable of being known, it follows that not only all possible *experience* of objects, but also all possible *objects* of experience, all possible objects of any sensible intuition, must conform to categories. These concepts lay down the form of all possible experience and so, given transcendental idealism, the form of all possible objects of sensible intuition.

That concludes my very quick summary of the connecting arguments of the Transcendental Deduction. How *particular* categories make possible the experience of objects in our, spatio-temporal, intuition is taken up in the Principles of Pure Understanding. When we have looked at the way Kant thinks that this is achieved – at least for three of the most important categories – we will flesh out the summary of the Transcendental Deduction.

# The Principles of Pure Understanding

*(A 148/B 187–A 235/B 294)*
Since everything that we (human beings) can experience – including everything that we can experience in space – is always conceived as existing in *time*, Kant now narrows his focus. He considers how the categories are to be applied specifically to temporal intuition; and, hence, to *everything* that can be, for us, an object of experience, an object that can exist in space and/or time. When the categories are applied to what comes in temporal intuition, they give rise to a set of necessary and universal rules which Kant calls 'the principles of pure understanding'. And he seeks to prove that, from the side of thought, these principles do, indeed, make our experience possible.

Although the section dealing in detail with these principles is divided into four subsections, it is the third, the Analogies of Experience, to which Kant himself says that his readers should pay special attention. The Analogies deal with the fundamental *dynamical* laws – the fundamental laws of behaviour – governing all the objects of nature. The vast majority of commentators have agreed with Kant in regarding the arguments of the three Analogies as central for assessing his claim that the categories make our own, spatio-temporal, experience possible. I see no reason for dissenting from this view. If we can understand why Kant thinks that the category of *substance* makes possible our consciousness of duration, the category of *cause* makes possible our experience of an object changing its state, and the category of *community* makes possible our experience of objects coexisting, we will have grasped the nub of his case for declaring that the categories are necessary for our experience, for our perceptual knowledge of spatio-temporal objects.

Rather confusingly (given there are three Analogies), Kant maintains that there are only *two* ways in which temporal experience is possible. We can either experience an object *changing its state* (discussed in the Second Analogy) or objects *coexisting* (discussed in the Third Analogy) – or, of course, we can have both types of experience together. However, in each case, the experience takes place *in* time. It is in the First Analogy that Kant discusses how we can have the thought of a *temporal span* or *duration*: a consciousness that is required for us to experience any change of state or coexistence (simultaneous existence) of objects.

In the case of all three Analogies, Kant is taking it for granted that we do experience objective change and coexistence (and so we are conscious of duration or a length of time). He is not attempting to prove that these temporal experiences occur, but to explain *how* they are possible. Accordingly, it is no objection to his strategy to point out that he here assumes that we experience objects changing their states and/or coexisting, and that he then argues from these experiences to the conditions that make them possible.

# First Analogy

*(A 182/B 224–A 189/B 232)*

The principle to be proved in the First Analogy is that, in all change of appearances, the quantity of substance in nature remains the same. (This principle is held to arise when the category of *substance* is applied to what is given in temporal intuition.)

Kant claims – correctly, I suggest – that we think of everything we experience, or can experience, as existing within one *continuous* temporal span, one temporal continuum (see e.g. the Anticipations of Perception, A 166/B 207–A 176/B 218). Although, for convenience, we can divide any length of time into smaller parts, e.g. a day into hours, and hours into minutes, each part is always conceived

as itself made up of an *extended* period. In short, we think that
between any two moments within a temporal span, there is always
a length of time. But how can our conception of time as a temporal
continuum be possible, given that all we are ever immediately
conscious of, through sensibility, is a manifold of *discretely* apprehended representations?

One suggestion might be that we acquire this conception of a
length of time or duration simply through a succession of representations being presented in intuition. But Kant sees a difficulty
with this. He does not deny that the presentation of successive
representations is necessary to form our notion of duration, but
he does deny that succession *on its own* can be sufficient. As
he puts it, 'in bare succession existence is always vanishing and
recommencing, and never has the least magnitude' (A 183/B 226).
He thinks that without the thought of something *permanent* to
which successive existences can be attributed, the conception of a
temporal magnitude, a duration, would be impossible. Our idea of
a length of time cannot be acquired through the mere successive
apprehension of discrete existences because, without the thought
of something permanent *connecting* these existences, he does not
believe that we could form our notion of a single temporal period
within which all these existences can be placed. He illustrates his
argument most perspicuously in the penultimate paragraph of the
First Analogy. He starts by assuming what he is going to rule out,
namely that there *could* be 'bare succession', or the absolute going
out of and coming into existence of objects. He then shows that, in
the field of appearances, such a hypothesis is impossible, because
there could be no recognition of a temporal continuum within
which alone the absolute going out of existence and the absolute
coming into existence could be perceived:

A coming to be or ceasing to be that is not simply a determination [a state] of the permanent but is absolute, can never be
a possible perception. For this permanent is alone what makes
possible the representation of the transition from one state to
another, and from not-being to being. These transitions can be
empirically known only as changing determinations [states] of
that which is permanent. If we assume that something absolutely
begins to be, we must have a point of time in which it was not.
But to what are we attach this point, if not to what already

exists? For a preceding empty time is not an object of perception. But if we connect the coming to be with things that previously existed, and which persist in existence up to the moment of this coming to be, this latter must be simply a determination [a state] of what is permanent in that which precedes it. Similarly also with ceasing to be; it presupposes the empirical representation of a time in which an appearance no longer exists.

*(A 188/B 231)*

The upshot is that, since we do have the experience of change, we need to recognize that all change must simply be a change of *state* of what remains or is permanent. We can never experience a change that is absolute, i.e. where the first object of perception absolutely ceases to be and is replaced with a second such object that absolutely comes into existence (*ex nihilo*). For if that were a possible experience, it would mean that there must have existed a period of time, however small, in which *nothing* could have been perceived to happen. This is so because, unless there were a perceived period of what Kant calls 'empty time' (a temporal period in which nothing can be perceived to happen), the *apparently* experienced absolute coming to be of the second object would merely be the experience of the *continuation* of what already existed (although in an earlier state). Since time is a continuum, there is always, between any two moments of time, a period of time. Hence, it would not be possible for the first object to be experienced to cease absolutely to exist, and the second object to be experienced absolutely to come into existence, *without* empty time.

Consequently, either the apparent coming into existence of the second object must be thought of as, in reality, a merely changing *state* of the first object (which never was, therefore, experienced absolutely to go out of existence) or there must have been a *period of time* which could, in principle, be perceived between the experience of the absolute going out of existence of the first object and that of the absolute coming into existence of the second object. The second alternative – the awareness of a temporal period between the annihilation of the first and the creation of the second object – is not, however, possible. It is not because, as Kant puts it, 'empty time is not an object of perception'; that is, without the perception of *something happening*, there can be no awareness of a temporal period or duration. Therefore, all change must be experienced as merely a change of state of what is permanent (substance). Neither the absolute going out of existence nor the absolute coming into existence of objects can possibly be experienced – since such alleged perceptions, by requiring a period of 'empty time', would flout the very temporal condition in which change can be experienced. Unless change is thought of as change of state (of what is permanent throughout), and not the absolute going out of existence of one object and the absolute coming into existence of another object in its stead, there could be no temporal period – no length of time – within which any change could be experienced. And since the objects of possible experience are appearances, and not things in themselves, it follows that given there can be no experience of the substance out of which spatio-temporal objects are composed being absolutely created or destroyed, no such creation or destruction of substance can take place. (Of course, tables and suns, for example, *can* 'cease to exist' in an everyday sense – the former by being e.g. reduced to pulp and the second by exploding – but, on Kant's argument, the *substance* of which they are composed must remain. Similarly, when we talk of spatio-temporal objects being 'created' or 'brought into existence', this 'creation' must be wholly utilizing a quantity of substance that *already* exists.)

In the First Analogy, Kant has argued that a fundamental principle lying at the basis of (Newtonian) natural science – viz. that all changes are merely changes of state of what remains throughout (substance) – is a justified synthetic a priori judgement. Although the denial of that judgement is not self-contradictory (so it is synthetic), it must always obtain (so it is a priori). It must always obtain because it is a condition of our consciousness of a temporal span, a duration, within which any change or coexistence among appearances can alone be experienced. Moreover, since, in sensibility, we are merely presented with a manifold of discrete representations, it follows that it is the *understanding* that makes possible our consciousness of duration or a length of time. It does so by connecting a manifold apprehended through sensibility by means of the category of *substance*, thereby making possible the experience of alteration (an object changing its state) – and, with it, the consciousness of duration. Without this action of the understanding, no empirical consciousness of change or coexistence could occur.

The two subsequent Analogies build on this foundation of the necessary permanence of substance. In the Second Analogy, it is maintained that all change must not only occur to what is permanent (as the First Analogy has argued) – and, hence, that every change is a change of state of what remains throughout – but that every change of state must itself occur according to the law of causality (alternatively entitled 'the principle of sufficient reason'). In brief, that every change of state, every event, must have a cause. (On Kant's terminology, 'an event' means the same as 'a change of state'). In the Third Analogy, it is maintained that all objects, in so far as they are coexisting in space must be in mutual causal connection; that is, accord with the law of community (alternatively entitled 'the principle of coexistence'). If Kant can succeed in proving these two subsequent Analogies, in addition to the First Analogy, he will have shown that everything in nature, everything in the spatio-temporal world, must be in thoroughgoing causal connection.

## Second Analogy

*(A 189/B 232–A 211/B 256)*
The principle to be proved in the Second Analogy is that all altera-tions or changes of state take place in conformity with the law of causality – or, more succinctly, that every event must have a cause. (This principle is held to arise when the category of *cause* is applied in temporal intuition.)

In order to explain how Kant seeks to prove the principle, let us concentrate on his two contrasting examples: the first is an example of experiencing an object changing its state and the second is an example of experiencing the coexisting parts of an (unchanging) object. As regards the first, he considers the perception of a boat moving off downstream by means of the apprehension of successive representations (from a boat upstream to a boat downstream). And as regards the second, he considers the perception of the coexisting parts of a house by means of the apprehension of successive repre-sentations (from the roof of a house to the basement of a house).

Now the question is: what is the condition that enables an observer to have the experience of an object changing its state rather than the experience of the coexisting parts of a stable object,

given that, in *both* cases, the manifold constituting the two appearances (boat going downstream, on the one hand, and the parts of a
house, on the other) are successively apprehended? Here is the *first*
part of Kant's answer:

> [I]n an appearance which contains a happening (the preceding
> state of the perception we may entitle A, and the succeeding B)
> B can be apprehended only as following upon A; the perception
> of A cannot follow upon B but only precede it. For instance,
> I see a boat move downstream. My perception of its lower
> position follows upon the perception of its position higher up
> in the stream, and it is impossible that in the apprehension of
> this appearance the boat should first be perceived lower down
> in the stream and afterwards higher up. The order in which
> the perceptions succeed one another in apprehension is in this
> instance determined, and to this order apprehension is bound
> down. In the ... example of a house my perceptions could begin
> with the apprehension of the roof and end with the basement, or
> could begin from below and end above ... In the series of these
> perceptions there was no determinate order specifying at what
> point I must begin in order to connect the manifold empirically.
> *(A 192/B 237–A 193/B 238)*

In other words, if I am to have the experience of an object
changing its state from A to B, my apprehension of the manifold
must be thought of as appropriately determined by the order in
the manifold itself, i.e. if the change is from state A to state B,
then, under normal circumstances, I must apprehend the states in
that order. So, if I am to have the consciousness of an objective
change from A to B, it is not enough that the representations of
the manifold, A and B, should, as a matter of fact, be successively
apprehended in that order; it is also necessary that I can think of
the manifold as *determining* my apprehension in a given way (in
a way that appropriately matches the order of the change in the
spatio-temporal world, i.e. from state A to state B).

But – and here is the *second* part of Kant's answer – this
thought is only possible if I can recognize that the manifold *itself*
is connected according to a certain rule, viz. a rule that necessitates
my apprehending, under the given circumstances, B after A. But
no such rule is given to me merely through *sensibility*: through the

mere apprehension of a manifold, I am simply conscious that, *as a matter of fact*, the representation B follows the representation A. The only alternative is for the *understanding* to provide the rule; and, among its rules, there is only one that could supply the required recognition. This is the law of causality (the principle of sufficient reason). By applying this law to the apprehended manifold, I am enabled to think that there is something in the circumstances of A such that whenever A occurs, under those circumstances, B must follow. Once the understanding has applied that rule to the manifold, I can recognize that, on this present occasion, my apprehension of B must follow my apprehension of A – and, hence, that I am experiencing a change in the object from A to B.

After all, through mere apprehension of a sensible manifold, the representations of that manifold are *always* apprehended successively, whatever type of objective state of affairs I am perceiving (or even if I am having no objective perception at all). Consequently, if I am to perceive the manifold as an objective *change*, something needs to be *added* to the successive apprehension of the manifold, thereby enabling me to recognize that, in this particular case, my apprehension is bound down by the succession in the manifold. It is the thought that the manifold is itself subject to the law of causality that provides the required recognition. The application of that law alone enables me to recognize that my apprehension of the manifold is appropriately *determined* in its order, i.e. that under the circumstances, my apprehension of B *must* follow my apprehension of A and that these apprehensions *cannot* be reversed.

In terms of Kant's example of a boat going downstream, let us assume that, on a given occasion, I apprehend through sensibility the representation of a boat upstream followed by the representation of a boat downstream. This successive apprehension of a manifold does not, by itself, enable me to know that I am witnessing an *objective* change, a boat going downstream. For that, I need to recognize that the order of my apprehension is, on this occasion, bound down to that order by the succession in the manifold. It is the recognition that, on this occasion, my apprehension of a boat downstream *had* to follow my apprehension of a boat upstream that enables me to grasp that I am perceiving an objective change (a succession that exists *distinct* from my apprehension, and that is why the apprehension, on that occasion, is bound down to that order and cannot be reversed). The only way in which this recognition can take place is by the understanding applying the law of causality to the succession in apprehension, thereby giving rise to the thought that there is something in the circumstances of the boat upstream such that, whenever any similar boat is in the same circumstances, it must go downstream. Once my understanding has combined the manifold by means of this law, I can think of my apprehension of the successive representations, on the given occasion, as bound down to that order. It is in this way, and this way alone, that I can experience a boat going downstream from the apprehended manifold of representations.

Given that the objects of the senses are appearances, we can now summarize the argument of the Second Analogy. It is the recognition that a manifold of sensible intuition is governed by a particular universal rule, the law of causality, which alone makes possible the experience of that manifold as an object changing its state. This synthetic a priori rule, the law of causality, is supplied by the understanding (employing, within the law, the category of *cause*) and applied to the manifold. Unless the manifold conforms to this law, no experience of a change of state is possible; and since spatio-temporal objects are appearances, it follows that every change of state in the spatio-temporal world, every event in nature, must be subject to the law of causality.

## Objections to the Second Analogy

1. The first of the two objections that I shall consider depends on the possibility that the temporal order of the event experienced can be different from the order of the experience of that event. Although, the objection concedes, it is normally the case that, with the experience of an objective change, the apprehension of the states of the change follows the same order as the change itself, there is no necessity here. If there were a craftily rigged up set of mirrors, it is conceivable that, even in the case of a boat going downstream, the subject would perceive the boat downstream first and (via the mirrors) the boat upstream second. In general, there is no unbreakable requirement that for the experience of a change of state, the order of apprehension should follow the order in the appearance. But, the objection concludes, the argument of the Second Analogy depends on the purported requirement that, in any

experience of change, the order of apprehension must follow the order in the appearance. I agree that there is no such requirement, and for the reason given in the objection; but, as we shall see, this fails to invalidate the argument.

The nub of Kant's argument is that, on any occasion of the experience of a change of state, the order of the manifold of representations must be conceived as *determining* the order of apprehension in a particular way, viz. by determining that this order is *irreversible*. Under normal circumstances, this has the consequence that the order of apprehension follows the same order as the change itself. But exceptional circumstances can, of course, be envisaged where apprehension of the second state occurs *before* apprehension of the first (as in the mirrors example). Nevertheless, it remains true that 'the order in which the perceptions (in the apprehension of this appearance) follow one another is a *necessary* order' (A 193/B 238; italics original). If I am experiencing an objective change of state, then how I apprehend the representations is not, on that occasion, *arbitrary* or *reversible*; and it *is* dependent on what happens (e.g. boat going downstream) being subject to the law of causality. However, in the *unusual* circumstances envisaged, I must apprehend the representations in the reverse order to the change itself (if I did not, I could not, on that occasion, have been experiencing the boat going downstream). Yet, if I am to recognize the manifold as disclosing, on that occasion, a particular change of state (a boat going downstream), I need to think that my apprehension is bound down in its order: I need to think that my apprehension of a boat upstream had to follow my apprehension of a boat downstream. Accordingly, I need to recognize that there is something in the circumstances surrounding the boat upstream such that, whenever it recurs under the same circumstances, the boat must go downstream (i.e. that the event of the boat going downstream falls under the law of causality) – and that is why, in the *unusual* circumstances, I must apprehend the boat downstream before I apprehend it upstream. Bringing in unusual surrounding circumstances has no affect on Kant's essential point, which (to repeat) is that in order to experience a change of state, the manifold must be thought of as subject to the law of causality. Without this act of thought, the subject could not recognize that the order of its apprehension is 'a *necessary* order', and so could not have the experience of a change of state.

2. The second objection – often referred to as the *non-sequitur* objection – was frequently made in the twentieth century, and by some of the very ablest of Kant's critics. In effect, Kant is accused of committing a stunning logical error. From the correct observation that, on any given occasion of experiencing a change of state, my apprehension must be appropriately determined or necessitated by the experienced change, Kant directly moves (it is alleged) to the wholly unjustified inference that it is necessary that the same change must be experienced to occur under *all* similar circumstances.

Suppose I experience water freezing on one occasion. This justifies me in holding that my apprehension is, on that occasion, determined in its order. (Assuming no mirrors and so on, this justifies me in holding that, on the given occasion, I must apprehend water in the liquid state followed by water in the solid state.) So far so good, the critics say. But it is wholly illegitimate to infer directly from this observation that *whenever* I perceive water in the liquid state, on any other relevantly similar occasion, it must be possible for me to perceive water solidify. The inference is a flagrant *non-sequitur*, which trades on the ambiguity in the meaning of 'determined' and 'necessitated'. From the fact that a subject's apprehension is, on a given occasion, determined or necessitated in its order by the experienced change of state, it does *not* follow that the *same* change, and consequently the same perception of change, will be determined or necessitated to recur on any other – let alone *every* other – similar occasion. For all that has been shown, there is nothing to prevent the water from *boiling*, and from being experienced to boil, on any other similar occasion. After all, suppose that water *did* boil on another similar occasion, it would still have been the case that on the first occasion (when the water froze), my apprehension of the change of state was, on that occasion, *determined* by the order in the world. It is manifest, therefore, that one cannot infer that the law of causality must apply to all changes of state, and so to all possible experience of such changes, from the correct observation that, on any occasion where a subject does experience a change of state, the subject's apprehension of that change is, on *that* occasion, appropriately determined or necessitated in its order by the change itself.

This well-known objection does not take proper account of Kant's idealism. Agreed, if the spatio-temporal world existed *in itself* – that is, independently of our capacity to experience it – the objection would be forceful. In *that* case, there would clearly be no inference from a subject's apprehension, on a given occasion, being determined in its order by the change of state to the change of state *itself* (and, consequently, the perception of it) necessarily *recurring* on every other similar occasion. As Kant himself puts it: 'How things may be in themselves, apart from the representations through which they affect us, is entirely outside our sphere of knowledge' (A 190/B 235). But his argument is directed to spatio-temporal objects *when conceived as appearances*. So conceived, the world of spatio-temporal objects does not exist independently of our capacity to know or experience it. Rather, we construct this world from the manifold of representations (mind-dependent phenomena) given to us through sensibility.

How, then, do we come to interpret some series of representations as manifesting an object changing its state? The central concern of the Second Analogy is precisely to answer this question. Without repeating the whole argument again, the line of Kant's answer is that: a) we need to think of our apprehension as appropriately determined for the experience of a change of state to occur; b) there is nothing in the manifold or series of representations, as this is given to us through sensibility, to enable us to grasp that our apprehension is appropriately determined; therefore c) our understanding needs to apply a suitable universal rule to that series of representations, in order for us to recognize that our apprehension is appropriately determined or necessitated by the representations. Without submitting the manifold to a suitable rule (the law of causality: the only suitable law among the principles of pure understanding), we could never think of the serial representations as appropriately determining our apprehension; and, hence, we could never experience this manifold as a change of state. Furthermore, unless such an experience is possible, it follows – given Kant's idealism – that no change of state can occur. In the field of appearances, therefore, every change of state, every event, must be subject to the law of causality.

The great value of the *non-sequitur* objection is that it emphasizes the centrality of Kant's Copernican revolution – and so his idealism – to his overall critical system. Kant is quite clear that there would be no hope of answering Humean scepticism about causation, and, more generally, of putting metaphysics, so far as that is possible, on the secure path of a science, *unless* his idealism is embraced. Indeed, it is one of his strongest criticisms of transcendental realism that it cannot provide a secure foundation for natural science and mathematics, unlike transcendental idealism. Paradoxically, it is those very critics who accuse Kant of committing a logical howler in the Second Analogy who have themselves been guilty of foisting upon him the position, transcendental realism, which he is precisely seeking to rebut – and rebut on the grounds that, if the standpoint of transcendental realism is adopted, no such argument as the one which he has employed in the Second Analogy could possibly succeed.

# Third Analogy

*(A 211/B 256–A 218/B 265)*
The Third Analogy attempts to prove the principle that all objects that can be perceived to coexist in space are in mutual causal connection. (This is the principle that arises when the category of *community* is applied to temporal intuition.)

Whereas, in the Second Analogy, Kant seeks to explain how the category of *cause*, and its corresponding principle (the law of causality), makes possible our experience of objective change, in the Third Analogy, he seeks to explain how the category of *community*, and its corresponding principle (the law of community or reciprocity), makes possible our experience of the coexistence of objects by means of successive perceptions.

Once again, the point he emphasizes is that for the requisite experience to be possible – here, the experience of objects coexisting – we need to recognize that our successive apprehension of the manifold is appropriately *determined* in its order. In particular, I cannot experience two objects, X and Y, coexisting – two entities that I think of as existing distinct from my apprehension and throughout a period of time at least equal to this apprehension – unless I can recognize that, at any moment during my apprehension of the manifold, I could have apprehended the representations of that manifold in the *reverse* order. For instance, if, by means of successive perceptions, I am experiencing the earth and moon coexisting over a given period then, although my apprehension of the earth and moon may, as it happens, have begun with a perception of the earth and been succeeded by a perception of the moon, it must have been possible to have perceived the moon, when I perceived the earth, and vice versa. It is, Kant holds, the recognition that the order of my apprehension could have been reversed, at any moment during my apprehension of the manifold, which alone enables me to think that while my *apprehension* of the manifold is successive, *what* I am apprehending is not in succession but coexisting in space.

But now the question arises as to how this recognition of reversibility can arise. While I may find that, following my apprehension of a succession of representations (X succeeded by Y), I can, at the next moment, proceed to reverse that order (Y succeeded by X), I evidently cannot recognize, merely through my apprehending a manifold through sensibility, that the order of apprehension could have been reversed at *any* moment of my alleged experience of coexistence. Yet, without this recognition of the reversibility of my apprehension, I cannot perceive the manifold as disclosing two coexisting objects, X and Y. Something, therefore, has to be added to the mere apprehension of the succession of representations; and, Kant contends, that addition is the thought that the contents of the apprehended representations are in *mutual* causal connection throughout a period of time which is at least equal to that of my apprehension of the manifold. Once the successively apprehended representations have been thus conceived to be in mutual causal connection, I can recognize that my apprehension could have been reversed at any moment during my apprehension of the successive representations; and, hence, that I am experiencing two objects coexisting in space.

Put briefly, it is the recognition that my apprehension of a succession of representations could, at any point during the apprehension, have been reversed that enables me to experience a coexistence of objects on the basis of the apprehended succession. This recognition is itself made possible by thinking of these representations as *mutually* causally connected, i.e. by the understanding applying *the law of community or reciprocity* to the succession of representations. It is, Kant holds, only through this employment of the understanding that the experience of objective coexistence can arise by means of the apprehension of a succession of representations. From which it further follows that, since the objects of the senses are appearances, and not things in themselves, all possible objects coexisting in space must be subject to the law of community or reciprocity.

(Of course, in the case of very distant, and widely separated, bodies – like two coexisting stars in two different galaxies from our own – there will be a considerable time lag before the light emanating from each star reaches the observer's eyes on earth. Nonetheless, if the observer is to experience these stars as coexisting on the basis of a succession of representations, the successive acts of perceptual apprehension must be thought of as reversible throughout the experience of coexistence. Although the experience of coexistence here occurs at a much later time than the states of the coexisting objects experienced (and these objects may even have ceased to exist by the time of the experience), the experience, and so the possibility of there being two objects coexisting (earlier), does require the thought that there is mutual causal connection between the objects. Consequently, the application of the law of community or reciprocity to the apprehended representations remains a condition for the experience of coexistence, even in the case of very remote and widely separated objects.)

## Two key points about the Analogies

First point:
A question that naturally arises from our discussion of the Analogies is how the subject comes to *apply* a particular category (rather than some other, or none) to a given manifold. Some commentators have taken it that, on Kant's view, the role of the understanding is to rearrange a mass of *chaotically* given representations into an orderly spatio-temporal universe by applying the categories to this chaos. Of course, this interpretation totally fails to explain *how* it comes about that a particular category is applied to a certain manifold and not to another. But the fact remains that some of Kant's own comments have encouraged the idea that he thinks that it is we ourselves, through the application of the categories, who have introduced order *by rearranging a chaotically given manifold*. Thus, near the end of the A edition of the Transcendental Deduction, he writes:

> Thus the order and regularity in the appearances, which we entitle *nature*, we ourselves introduce. We could never find them in the appearances, had not we ourselves, or the nature of our mind originally set them there.
>
> *(A 125; italics original)*

Nonetheless, it is a serious mistake to regard such comments as showing that, on Kant's view, our understanding processes an essentially chaotically given manifold into an orderly series of representations. Rather, his point is that since we must be able to grasp the manifold as falling under (strictly) *universal and necessary* rules if we are to have any experience, any sensible knowledge of objects, the entirely law-abiding nature of objects cannot be derived *from* our perception of nature – since no universal and necessary rules can be discovered through perception alone – but must be put there by *ourselves*, i.e. through the application of the categories to the manifold of representations. That is why he immediately goes on from the passage just quoted:

> For this unity of nature has to be a necessary one, that is, has to be an a priori certain unity of the connection of appearances; and such synthetic unity could not be established a priori if there were not subjective grounds of such unity contained a priori in the original cognitive powers of our mind [viz. the pure concepts of the understanding], and if these subjective conditions, inasmuch as they are the grounds of the possibility of knowing any object whatsoever in experience, were not at the same time objectively valid.
>
> *(A 125/6)*

But the categories could not be applied, in the first place, unless the given manifold *itself* possessed the type of order that made such application possible. Kant is certainly not claiming that experience is possible even though the manifold, as it is presented in our forms of sensible intuition, is constituted by a chaotic succession of representations. On the contrary, it is a particular order of representations, repeatedly apprehended through sensibility, which fixes whether the category of *cause* or *community* is to be applied to an apprehended manifold: see e.g. *Prolegomena*, Sect. 29. But, as we have just noted, consciousness of the order of a manifold, as it is apprehended through sensibility, is never enough to make experience possible, because there is, as yet, no thought of one's apprehension being *bound down* or *determined* in a specific way – and, hence, no thought of an *object* of the senses can arise. It is the work of the understanding, together with its categories, which makes possible this thought of an object; and it does so precisely by submitting the manifold to universal and necessary rules. Such rules, however, could not be employed unless the order in the manifold itself conforms to these rules.

What Kant is resisting is the view – which he ascribes to Hume – that it is merely a *contingent* feature of the spatio-temporal world (nature) that its objects are in thoroughgoing causal determination; and that it could have been the case that we found this world to be in chaos or confusion, or that (given it is not, as a matter of fact) we might find it to become so at any future moment. No such alleged experience is possible, Kant is claiming, once it is acknowledged that the objects of the senses are appearances and not things in themselves. Spatio-temporal objects must be in thoroughgoing causal determination in order for experience to be possible; and this requires that we must be able to recognize that the manifold of representations, as it is given to us through sensibility, conforms to (strictly) universal rules employing the categories of our understanding.

Second point:
It needs to be stressed that in claiming to have shown that the laws of causality and community, together with the principle of the permanence of substance, are the basic synthetic a priori dynamical principles governing the spatio-temporal world, Kant is not claiming to have any a priori knowledge of what, *in particular*, the causes of any phenomena are (and, analogously, *what* substance is permanent throughout any change). For example, Kant thinks that what are the *empirical* causes of the boat going downstream and what are the *empirical* mutual causal relations between the earth and moon must remain entirely a matter for scientific investigation. What is alone being claimed is that we can know a priori that there is *some* causal relationship or mutual causal connection governing these respective objective states of affairs (boat going downstream, on the one hand, and the coexistence of the earth and moon, on the other). And, of course, the same point goes for any other change of state or coexistence of objects. However, any claim to have located what the specific empirical causes of any given type of phenomena are will always, from our point of view, have the status of a synthetic *a posteriori* judgement. It is merely the pure laws (or principles) of causality and community that are wholly synthetic a priori. Neither is true in virtue of the meaning of the terms involved (hence they are both *synthetic* judgements); and yet the law of causality must apply to *any* objective change of state and the law of

community to *any* coexistence between objects (hence they are both *a priori* – since necessity and universality are two sure criteria of the a priori). No instance of these temporal phenomena – an objective change of state or an objective coexistence – can be experienced unless the respective principle is applicable to the manifold of representations. In respect of these experiences, therefore, the laws of causality and community must obtain.

# Back to the Transcendental Deduction

I said earlier that a grasp of the argument of the Analogies should help us to understand the (highly abstract) Transcendental Deduction. I must now try to make good this claim.

An essential point to draw from the Analogies is that if a subject is to perceive a manifold of representations as a temporal appearance, the successive representations, constituting the given manifold, must be synthesized or connected (by the understanding) in conformity with categories, and hence must together conform to universal rules. The synthesis must be in accordance with universal rules because in no other way can the subject think of its *apprehension* of the manifold as bound down or necessitated; and without this thought no experience of any object existing in time, by means of that manifold, is possible. It is the subject's recognition that its apprehension is bound down or necessitated in a specific way that makes possible its experience of a particular type of object or objective state of affairs. (For instance, it is the subject's recognition that its apprehension of a succession of representations is bound down to that order – by the understanding's application of the law of causality to the apprehended manifold – that makes possible the subject experiencing the manifold as an object *changing its state*.) As Kant puts it: 'The object is *that* in the appearance which contains the condition of this necessary rule of apprehension' (A 191/B 236; italics original).

In brief, the Analogies explain how specific categories, by bringing a manifold of temporal intuition to the unity of consciousness, make possible a particular type of experience in time. More specifically, by conceiving the separately given representations of a temporal manifold as governed by the category of *cause* or *community*, the subject is enabled to connect the serial representations in *one* act of temporal consciousness, viz. by thinking of them as forming, on the one hand, *an object changing its state* or as forming, on the other, *a coexistence of objects*. Further, unless relational categories (*substance, cause* or *community*) can be applied to a manifold, no knowledge of any object existing in time can occur by means of this manifold. For if none of these categories apply to a manifold of temporal intuition, this means that the manifold cannot be thought in one act of temporal consciousness: it cannot since these categories, when applied to our temporal form of intuition, provide an exhaustive set of rules for enabling us to think of a manifold as forming *any* determinate relation in time (as an enduring object, as an objective change of state, or as a coexistence of objects). But if a manifold cannot be thought in one act of temporal consciousness, no single subject can be conscious of all the representations of the manifold as existing together in time; and, hence, there can be no subject who, on the basis of that manifold, can be conscious of any object existing in time. Since all objects existing in time are merely appearances, it follows that if no single subject can be *conscious* of any object in time, no temporal object (and so, too, no object in space) can *exist*.

By grasping how the categories of *substance, cause* and *community* make our – temporal – experience possible, I submit that we can now appreciate much more clearly why Kant holds, in the Transcendental Deduction, that the categories make experience possible in any sensible form of intuition whatever. They do so because only in so far as categories can be applied to a manifold of sensible intuition can one subject be conscious of all the representations of that manifold. The fundamental condition for knowledge of a manifold of representations to arise, viz. that *one* subject must be conscious of *all* the (separately apprehended) representations of that manifold, itself entails that such knowledge is only possible if these representations can be combined in *one* thought, in *one* act of consciousness. With respect to any manifold of sensible intuition, the capacity to combine the representations in one act of consciousness is only possible in so far as the manifold can be recognized as conforming to categories. For the categories are the mind's fundamental and exhaustive ways of combining any manifold of sensible intuition into a unified intuition (and, hence, of conceiving the manifold in one act of consciousness). For instance, in the case of temporal intuition, the category of *cause*, when applied to the representations of a manifold, makes possible the consciousness of that manifold as a change of state. Here this category combines a manifold, given in the form of temporal intuition, into a single temporal unit, viz. into an appearance changing its state. Likewise, the category of *community*, when applied to a manifold of temporal intuition makes possible the consciousness of that manifold as a single temporal unit, though a different one, viz. into appearances coexisting.

Once it is accepted that for any manifold of sensible intuition to be collectively known, that manifold must conform to categories, we can see how our experience of any *object* of the senses is dependent on the categories. For an object of the senses is always conceived as determining us to apprehend the manifold, through which it is given, in a specific manner. (Thus, in the temporal case of experiencing an object changing its state or of experiencing objects coexisting, the subject's apprehension of the manifold is bound down by the disposition of the object: in the first case, the apprehension must be conceived as *irreversible* and, in the second case, as *reversible*). Accordingly, the very possibility of a subject perceiving any object of sensible intuition depends on the subject being able to think of the manifold, out of which it is composed, as determining or necessitating the way it is apprehended. Yet through sensibility, the representations of a manifold are simply presented separately in intuition: no thought of any *necessity* in the manner of apprehending the representations can arise through sensibility alone. Hence, if any manifold of representations is to be perceived as manifesting an object of sensible intuition, it must be the understanding which, by thinking of the manifold as governed by some universal and necessary rule(s), enables us to recognize that our apprehension is bound down. Since the categories are the understanding's most basic rules for combining or unifying representations, given in any form of sensible intuition, it follows that an object of sensible intuition can be known if, but only if the manifold can be thought in accordance with categories. Moreover, since all objects of sensible intuition can exist only in so far as they are capable of being known or experienced – they are consti- tuted by a manifold of representations combined by means of the categories – it further follows that all possible objects of sensible intuition must conform to the categories.

*

No doubt there are a number of serious questions that ought to be raised about the premises both of the Transcendental Deduction and of the proofs in the Principles of Pure Understanding. Two, especially, deserve scrutiny. First, has Kant really managed to show that the categories are an exhaustive list of the mind's ways of uniting any manifold of sensible intuition? Second, is he right to claim that space and time are to be equated with our forms of sensible intuition, and, hence, merely constitute properties of our mind? But given his premises, the central arguments in the Transcendental Deduction and Principles seem to me more difficult to fault than many philosophers have supposed.

# Refutation of [Problematic] Idealism

Although the Transcendental Deduction does not *directly* address scepticism about the very existence of objects of outer sense – that we have perceptual knowledge of such objects is assumed and the question is about how this experience is possible – Kant does later directly confront scepticism about the very existence of objects in space. He discusses this scepticism in the B edition of the *Critique of Pure Reason*, in a subsection of the Principles of Pure Understanding entitled 'Refutation of Idealism' (B 274–9), and at a number of other places, notably at B xxxix–xli and B 291–3. He also discusses it in the Fourth Paralogism of the A edition (A 366–80); but he does not there attempt to show that the Cartesian sceptic's position is self-refuting. For the most part, I shall confine my comments to the B-edition treatment.

Kant considers the position of the Cartesian sceptic or, as he also calls this type of sceptic, the 'problematic idealist'. (This is the sceptical position adopted by Descartes with respect to the subject's knowledge of spatial objects without a proof of a non-deceiving creator.) The Cartesian sceptic does not doubt his own *continued* existence, but does doubt the existence of objects in space. The grounds of the sceptic's doubt hinges on the assumption that *transcendental realism* is the correct description of the subject's relationship to objects in space (allowing for the moment that such objects exist). On this assumption, the sceptic argues that the existence of objects in space must be doubtful because we have to seek to *infer* the existence of objects outside us (and so in space) from data, serial representations, all of which exists in us (and so only in time). Such an inference can never be certain; it is *at best* only a probable one. For since, according to the transcendental realist, we can never have any immediate awareness of spatial objects – but only of the representations which these objects, if they exist, have produced in us – how do we know that the representations have not been caused by something entirely *different* from spatial objects, e.g. by a malignant (non-spatial) demon or by something within our own minds?

This, then, is the challenge posed by the Cartesian sceptic, the problematic idealist. Kant seeks to turn the tables on this sceptic by arguing that it would be demonstrably impossible to have a consciousness of oneself as a temporally extended subject (as it is agreed each of us does have), if the transcendental realist's conception of the relationship between this subject and objects in space were correct. Kant's argument hinges on the claim that if, as the transcendental realist affirms, everything we can sense immediately – i.e. non-inferentially – exists in us (understood as merely temporally extended beings), there would be nothing upon which to base the consciousness of a *length of time* or *duration*. There would not because all that would ever be encountered in inner intuition, by which the consciousness of duration could arise, is a manifold or series of *discrete* occurrences (representations); and these, by themselves, are insufficient for acquiring such consciousness. As Kant had remarked in the First Analogy, 'in bare succession existence is always vanishing and recommencing, and never has the least magnitude [duration]' (A 183/B 226). But if a series of representations, successively apprehended in inner intuition, is insufficient by itself to generate the consciousness of a length of time, it must be equally insufficient for the subject to have a consciousness of *itself* as extended in time, that is, as existing over a temporal period.

On the transcendental idealist's theory, however, objects in space are *immediately* – not mediately (inferentially) – perceived, i.e. they are *intuited*; and, Kant claims, it is perfectly possible, on this latter theory, to have the consciousness of a length of time or duration. It is made possible through the intuition of an object *changing its spatial position*: see B 277–8 and also B 291–3. By recognizing that one and the same object has moved through space, the subject can acquire the consciousness of a length of time, viz. the time in which the object has been observed to change its spatial position. Once the consciousness of a length of time has been formed by means of this outer intuition, the subject can, correspondingly, become conscious of its *own* existence as extended in time, viz. *during* the period (at least) when the object has been perceived to change its spatial position. In other words, we acquire the consciousness of ourselves as subjects extended in time by means of the immediate perception of an object changing its position in space. Since nothing is presented *in* us – that is, in *inner* intuition – except a succession of *un*connected representations (and such a 'bare succession' cannot provide us with the awareness of duration), the consciousness of temporal extension has to be derived from *outer* intuition. More specifically, the perceptual recognition that one and the same object has moved through space provides the subject with the consciousness of a *continuously* existing object; and thereby with the consciousness of its *own* continuous existence during that spatial experience. As a result, the successive apprehensions of this moving object come to be thought of as changing *states* – changing acts of awareness – of one and the same *persisting* subject.

Kant maintains, therefore, that the very condition that makes possible the Cartesian sceptic's consciousness of himself as an enduring or temporally extended subject proves that his scepticism about the existence of objects outside us – that is, *in space* – is impossible. At the same time, this proof shows that the Cartesian sceptic's theory of the relationship of the subject to its hoped-for objects in space, viz. transcendental realism, must be mistaken. According to that theory, immediate consciousness is inevitably constituted by a succession of disparate representations in us (conceived as temporally extended beings): there can be no non-inferential consciousness – that is, no *intuition* – of the space in which external objects are located. On the contrary, space and its objects (things in themselves, for the transcendental realist) are said to be inferred from the succession of representations apprehended in us. But this picture of the relationship between ourselves and objects in space must entail that there can be no possible consciousness of ourselves as extended in time. For although the transcendental realist *alleges* that we possess an immediate consciousness of ourselves as existing in time (but no immediate consciousness of objects existing in space), Kant has argued that the very possibility of our having any consciousness of ourselves as existing in time – as both the transcendental realist and idealist agree that we do have – *requires* our having an immediate, i.e. a non-inferential, perceptual consciousness of spatial objects. There could be no question of our having any consciousness of ourselves as existing in time, if we could only seek to infer the existence of objects in space from a succession of disparate representations presented in inner intuition. Without the immediate consciousness of an object's spatial movement, no consciousness of a length of time and so of the subject's consciousness of its own temporal existence (in experiencing the object moving in space) is possible.

It may seem that, in his Refutation of [Problematic] Idealism, Kant is going back on his previous, and often repeated, assertion that space exists only as a form of our sensibility and does not, therefore, exist distinct from the mind. But that is not so. When he claims that objects can be proved to exist 'outside us' in space, *we* are being conceived merely as subjects *existing in time*. His claim is that unless we can be immediately conscious of objects in *outer* intuition (space), we could not be conscious of ourselves as having an extended existence in *inner* intuition (time). He is not claiming that, in order to be conscious of ourselves as temporally extended subjects, we must be immediately conscious of *things in themselves*. It is quite impossible, even on the transcendental realist's view, to be immediately conscious of things in themselves. And, in any case, the expression 'outside us' when applied to things in themselves does not, for Kant, refer to anything in space – whereas the expression 'outside us' obviously does refer to space in his discussion of problematic idealism. As he had said in the Fourth Paralogism of the A edition: 'The expression "outside us" is thus unavoidably ambiguous in meaning, sometimes signifying what *as a thing in itself* exists apart from us, and sometimes what belongs to outer *appearance*. In order, therefore, to make this concept, in the latter sense ... quite unambiguous, we shall distinguish *empirically external* objects from those that may be said to be external in the transcendental sense [i.e. as things in themselves], by explicitly entitling the former "things which are to be found in space"' (A 373; italics original. See also *Prolegomena*, Section 49, where he reiterates these two senses of 'outside us'.). It is, of course, '*empirically external* objects' – objects that we can *sense* as external (and, therefore, as existing in space) – to which Kant is referring in his Refutation, and these are *outer appearances*, not things in themselves. Accordingly, in arguing there against the problematic idealist, he is not retracting his claim that space belongs only to the form of our sensibility, and that its objects are merely appearances. Rather, he is reaffirming his claim that spatial objects are appearances, and not things in themselves. For, he contends, only if they are, can we be conscious of ourselves as temporally extended beings.

Here is a summary of the main points of Kant's Refutation. As the Cartesian sceptic would have it, all that we (taken as beings existing in time) can ever be non-inferentially conscious of, by means of perception, is a series of discrete representations. On this view, while each of us allegedly knows of our own continued existence throughout this series of representations, our only way to acquire knowledge of objects existing in space outside us is by means of an inference from these serial representations in us (conceived as temporally extended beings) to their putative cause among *things in themselves*. Hence, on the Cartesian theory, objects in space are things in themselves and are, at best, mediately perceived. That is why the transcendental realist becomes a Cartesian sceptic or problematic idealist. Once the objects in space are regarded as things in themselves, we can have no certainty as to their existence (assuming we are not in possession of a valid proof of a non-deceiving God). As we have seen, Kant's reply is that we must have immediate, not mediate, perception of objects in space – more strictly, of an object *moving* through space – in order to have the consciousness of our own continued existence. The acknowledged consciousness of our own temporally extended existence precisely requires that objects in space are not things in themselves, but *appearances in outer sense*, that is, in outer sensible intuition.

# Concluding the Transcendental Analytic

I said at the opening of this chapter that, in the Transcendental Analytic, Kant sets out to explain how synthetic a priori judgements are possible in pure natural science. That is, he sets himself the task of explaining how it can be that we are in possession of the synthetic a priori laws lying at the very basis of natural science.

It has emerged that the principles of pure understanding – most importantly, those principles dealt with in the three Analogies of Experience – *are* the fundamental synthetic a priori laws governing the existence and behaviour of all possible spatio-temporal objects. For the principles of pure understanding specify the fundamental universal and necessary rules governing our possible experience of all spatio-temporal objects. Since spatio-temporal objects are merely appearances, these principles likewise state the basic rules governing the existence and behaviour of all possible spatio-temporal objects. They are, consequently, *equivalent to* the laws of pure natural science.

While the principles of pure understanding are neither true in virtue of the meaning of the terms involved (they are not analytic) nor capable of being proved by recourse to experience (they are not a posteriori), they *are* provable. For, as Kant has shown, these synthetic a priori principles must be applicable to the manifold of representations if any experience of spatio-temporal objects (appearances) is to be possible; and so, given Kant's idealism, for spatio-temporal objects themselves to exist. Thus, in the Second Analogy, it has been proved that the synthetic a priori principle 'Every event must have a cause' makes our experience of *objective change* possible. If we can have any experience of a spatio-temporal object changing its state, the given manifold must be governed by the principle of sufficient reason. Hence too, on Kant's idealism, a spatio-temporal object can only change its state in conformity with that principle.

In sum, we are in possession of the principles of pure understanding – and so, equivalently, the fundamental laws of natural science – precisely because they *make our experience, our perception of spatial-temporal objects, possible*. If these synthetic a priori laws (or principles) did *not* apply to what comes in spatio-temporal intuition, we could have no experience of objects in space and time and, consequently, no spatio-temporal objects could exist. That is the explanation of their possibility.

An analogous approach goes for explaining how the synthetic a priori judgements of mathematics can have *objective* validity, that is, hold for all possible *objects* in space or time. Although mathematical judgements concerning spatio-temporal objects are not necessary in virtue of the meaning of the terms involved, they are necessary for us to have any possible experience of these objects in respect of their structural form. Hence, too, they are necessary for all the objects that can exist in space or time. For the objects of the senses are appearances, not things in themselves. Accordingly, like space and time, they can exist only in our possible intuitions of them. Now mathematical judgements hold necessarily for the structure of our pure intuitions, and so for the structure of space and time (proved in the Transcendental Aesthetic). Since appearances are empirical intuitions, they must '[a]s intuitions in space and time ... be represented through the same synthesis whereby space and time in general are determined' (A 162/B 203). In other words, the synthetic a priori judgements of pure mathematics – which determine the structure of space and time – must *equally* determine spatio-temporal objects in respect of their structural form. For since spatio-temporal objects are merely appearances, they are each constructed from some given manifold of representations; and every manifold is given to us *in the form of* spatial and/ or temporal intuitions. Consequently, the same mathematical rules that apply to the formation of a *pure* intuition (in the construction of any mathematical proof) must equally apply to *empirical* intuition (in the perception or imagination of any object in nature). That is the explanation of how the synthetic a priori judgements of pure mathematics must apply not only to the structure of space and time, but to all the possible objects of our experience, to all the objects that can exist in space or time.

*

If we allow that the Transcendental Analytic has proved that the categories make experience possible, and, more particularly, that the principles of pure understanding make our – spatio-temporal – experience possible, the following inference can be drawn and Kant draws it. Since these principles are, at the same time, the synthetic a priori laws lying at the basis of natural science, it follows that metaphysics in its *first* part – the part that is concerned with the foundations of our knowledge of nature – has been justified. For this knowledge has been proved to be based upon a priori concepts (the categories) that belong to our faculty of theoretical reason (which includes the understanding). And, on Kant's conception of *metaphysics*, if any a priori knowledge is to count as metaphysical knowledge, it must arise purely out of the mind's (a priori) faculty of theoretical reason. (That, incidentally, is why the synthetic a priori judgements of mathematics do not count, for Kant, as instances of metaphysical knowledge: since they require recourse to a priori *intuition*, they do not depend on our faculty of theoretical reason alone, but on our faculty of sensibility as well). In respect of the aim of metaphysics in its first part, therefore, Kant holds that his Copernican revolution in metaphysics has produced a very positive result. By showing that the laws of pure natural science depend on the mind's own a priori concepts (the categories), and that these categories themselves have been systematically and exhaustively deduced from the understanding's own judgement forms, metaphysics has been put onto the secure path of a science.

But it is also apparent that this positive result for metaphysics, in its first part, hinges on the objects of our possible experience being *appearances* and not things in themselves. It is the application of the categories to the representations given in spatio-temporal intuition that enables us to know objects (as appearances). So far as obtaining a priori knowledge in metaphysics concerning those objects that entirely *transcend* experience (and so sensible intuition) – the task of metaphysics in its second part – the outlook is distinctly less promising. It is less promising because the categories cannot be employed, for theoretical purposes, to characterize objects that transcend any possible sense experience. They cannot precisely because there will then be no sensible intuition with which the categories can *engage*, and thereby determine or characterize the objects *of* that sensible intuition. In other words, the categories are incapable of being employed *independently of* any sensible intuition in order to gain any theoretical knowledge of objects. It is only when they are applied to what is given in sensible intuition that they are enabled to determine or characterize any data for theoretical purposes. For instance, so far as human beings are concerned, the bare category of *cause* is provided with a determinate theoretical use by applying it to what is given in our *temporal* form of intuition. When so applied, it gives rise to the principle that every change of state – a temporal phenomenon – must have a cause. Quite generally, if, but only if, the categories are used *in conjunction with* some form of sensible intuition is it possible for them to determine data. (In the example, the category of *cause* is used to determine whether data that are presented in our temporal form of intuition constitute a change of state). From a theoretical point of view, therefore, the categories cannot be used to determine or characterize anything with regard to things in themselves because these are *never* presented in sensible intuition. Yet, together, the categories exhaustively comprise the mind's a priori concepts or ways of thinking about any data. Consequently, we can have no grounds for hoping that by merely exercising our theoretical reason, we can determine anything, positive *or* negative, about objects that transcend possible experience.

In the concluding chapter of the Analytic of Principles, Kant sets out, in summary fashion, why the positive results obtained by theoretical reason in regard to the objects of possible sense experience are *not* going to be repeated in regard to the objects that entirely transcend this experience. It is here that he introduces his well-known terminological distinction between phenomena and noumena, and prepares us for his detailed criticisms of the second part of metaphysics which he will undertake in the Transcendental Dialectic.

# The phenomena–noumena distinction

*(A 235/B 294–A 260/B 315)*

> Bereave matter of all its intelligible qualities, both primary and secondary, you in a manner annihilate it, and leave only a certain unknown, inexplicable *something*, as the cause of our perceptions [or representations]; a notion so imperfect, that no sceptic will think it worthwhile to contend against it.
>
> *(David Hume,* An Enquiry concerning Human Understanding, *Section XII, Part I)*

Before explaining his distinction between phenomena and noumena, Kant emphasizes the point made above, namely that the pure concepts of the understanding (the categories) need sensible intuition to give them any determinate meaning: the pure concepts of *substance, cause, community*, etc. acquire meaning and sense only *in conjunction with* sensible intuition (in our case, of course, this sensible intuition is spatio-temporal intuition). He is thus issuing a warning, in advance of his more narrowly focused criticisms in the Transcendental Dialectic, that it is simply wrong-headed to suppose that we can employ the categories in order to know anything determinate, by means of theoretical reason, about the ground or cause of the appearances, viz. things in themselves

– since this ground is, by its very nature, *not* an object of any sensible intuition.

However, in stressing this point, Kant also acknowledges that there are two ways in which we may attempt to think about things in themselves; and, in outlining how they differ, he employs some technical terms for the first time, although he will employ this terminology often enough hereafter. He refers to spatio-temporal objects (appearances) as 'phenomena' and things in themselves as 'noumena'; and, correspondingly, 'the phenomenal world' refers to the actual and possible objects of our senses taken as a whole, and the 'noumenal world' to the entire body of things in themselves, whether or not a particular thing in itself (or noumenon) is thought of as the ground of any appearance.

Now, within this terminology, Kant distinguishes between two senses in which talk of noumena could be taken: these he divides into noumena in the *negative* sense and noumena in the *positive* sense. He is emphatic that it is only talk in accordance with the former sense, the negative sense, which can be justified on the basis of theoretical reason – despite the fact that metaphysicians have repeatedly supposed that they are justified in making claims about noumena in the positive sense.

To talk about noumena in the *negative* sense is to acknowledge that the phenomenal world – the world that we know about by means of our understanding *and* sensibility – is *not* the only world that exists or may exist; and that it is not unreasonable, even from a theoretical point of view, to assume that there is an object (or a number of objects) that grounds or causes these appearances. Just because our theoretical knowledge is confined, and necessarily so (given our faculties of knowledge), to what is presented in sensible intuition, and so to a world of appearances, we should not assume that this is all that exists; and, more especially, we should not assume that the representations, out of which appearances (sensible entities) are constituted, have no cause or ground beyond the sensible world. In fact, Kant takes it as *certain* that noumena exist. And since these objects cannot be known by means of the senses, they must be objects of thought alone or, what he calls, 'intelligible entities':

Doubtless, indeed, there are intelligible entities corresponding to the sensible entities; there may also be intelligible entities to which our sensible faculty of intuition has no relation whatever; but our concepts of understanding, being mere forms of thought for our sensible intuition, could not in the least apply to them. That, therefore, which we entitle 'noumenon' must be understood as being such only in the *negative* sense.

*(B 308–9; italics original)*

In contrast to this negative – and legitimate – sense, if someone talks of noumena in the *positive* sense, this is to talk of noumena as though we have the theoretical capacity for *characterizing* or *describing* the intrinsic properties of these entities. And this, Kant holds, is entirely illegitimate. The only concepts that we possess for characterizing objects are the categories (and empirical concepts dependent on them). But these categories are empty of theoretical meaning *unless* they are applied to sensible intuition (and, in our case, spatio-temporal intuition). Since noumena are, *ex hypothesi, not* objects of sensible intuition, we cannot characterize them in any direct way. The best that we can do is to think about noumena in a purely *relative* way; that is, refer to them as those entities, whatever they are, which are the ground or cause of the phenomena. On analogy, *genes* were once identified simply as whatever are responsible for inheritance characteristics. The difference is that later observations and experiments have enabled us positively to characterize genes – to specify their chemical constitution and to understand *how* they bring about their effects – while it is *in principle* impossible for us to grasp the intrinsic nature of noumena by means of observation or theoretical reason.

Only if we possessed a type of understanding that is entirely *different* from our own – what Kant calls 'an intellectual intuition' – could we have any theoretical knowledge of what noumena are like. Such an understanding would be an intellectual one, like our own understanding, but which, unlike ours, would be sufficient *by itself* to characterize the intrinsic nature of noumena. Not only are we lacking any such capacity; we cannot even form a conception of what such a capacity would be like. In fact, Kant contends that such a capacity can probably only be ascribed to God or the 'primordial being' (see B 71–2).

It may seem surprising that, in the light of his diagnosis of why the metaphysician's attempts to establish the central claims of metaphysics – the claims that entirely transcend experience – are bound to fail, Kant should proceed, in the Dialectic, to take so much trouble to uncover the fallacies involved in their attempted proofs. Part of the reason is that the plausibility of his position is greatly enhanced if he can make good his general diagnosis in detail. That is, if he can show, case by case, that the arguments that have actually been employed by the metaphysician do fail for the reasons that his diagnosis, in the Analytic, has predicted, viz. that except where the categories are used to make experience possible (by being applied to sensible intuition), they can provide us with no theoretical knowledge. But there is a further reason. If it can be established that some of the metaphysical arguments concerning the noumenal world are in irresolvable *conflict* with one another, this must provide additional grounds for throwing out the metaphysician's claim to have access to the noumenal world by means of the sole method open to him, namely, theoretical reason.

Finally, it is vital to note, both with regard to his general comments here at the end of the Analytic and, even more, with regard to his detailed arguments in the upcoming Dialectic, that his critique of the metaphysician's attempts to talk about noumena in the *positive* sense is only intended to refer to the attempt to gain knowledge of noumena by means of *theoretical* reason. Despite any suggestion to the contrary, the restriction which Kant places on our possible a priori knowledge of objects, viz. that it is wholly limited to what can come in sensible intuition, is not intended to rule out the possibility that our *moral* experience, which includes the employment of *practical* reason, may be able to determine something positive about the noumenal world. As his second critique, the *Critique of Practical Reason*, testifies, he is confident that it will. At the same time, he will not renege on his critical claim that it is impossible for us to discover anything about the noumenal world which would provide us with the means of determining what the empirical world (nature), in regard to its specific content, is like. Nature is the province of the senses in conjunction with the understanding. And while we can, indeed must, possess certain synthetic a priori judgements in regard to nature's form – mathematical judgements and the principles of pure natural science – the a priori knowledge that our moral experience will provide us with can make no difference to our conception of the natural world as a thoroughgoing deterministic system, the specific (empirical)

knowledge of which can only be acquired through *sense experience*
and so a posteriori.

\*

But, now, it may be said that Kant's *idealism* must make it impossible for sense experience to provide us with any good reason for
believing in the existence of *other* sentient beings. Since, on his
theory, the objects that constitute nature (appearances) depend
for their existence on the spatial and temporal forms of (mind-
dependent) sensibility, how can I be certain that there exist any
other beings capable of conscious states? I will have to resort to
an *inference* from the appearances in my spatio-temporal forms
of intuition to the existence of other sentient beings existing
independent of my mind. Such an inference, as Kant himself
acknowledges, is *at best* a hazardous one. In short, Kant's transcendental idealism generates a serious sceptical problem concerning
the existence of other minds.

While it would be foolish to deny that transcendental idealism
does raise the sceptical problem of other minds, it is by no means
clear that this provides any ammunition for the rival theory of
our relation to the objects of the senses, namely transcendental
realism. The transcendental realist has to resort to an inference
even to claim to know of the existence of spatio-temporal objects,
*let alone* whether some of these spatio-temporal objects – more
particularly, human bodies – are animated (presumably a further
inference would be required to establish that sentience can be
ascribed to some spatio-temporal objects). Since, according to
the transcendental idealist, there are decisive reasons for rejecting
transcendental realism quite apart from the fact that it needs to
resort to an inference to seek to establish the objects of experience,
the problem of other minds – a problem which looks at least as
difficult for the transcendental realist as the idealist – cannot be a
reason for rejecting transcendental idealism in favour of the alternative theory.

# 3

# The Transcendental Dialectic: the limits of Pure Reason

In the Transcendental Dialectic, Kant shows in detail why it is that metaphysics in its second part – the part that deals with questions that transcend any possible sense experience – cannot provide us with any knowledge.

It is this part of metaphysics which deals with the three central questions of that discipline: the questions concerning the existence of God, freedom of the will, and the immortality of the soul. In addition, this part deals with some further questions which transcend any possible experience, viz. concerning the age and size of the spatio-temporal world as a whole and concerning the ultimate constituents of this world.

The Dialectic is divided into three main sections: first, the Paralogisms of Pure Reason, second, the Antinomy of Pure Reason, and third, the Ideal of Pure Reason. In these sections, Kant is primarily concerned to criticize the attempts by metaphysicians to establish, by the use of theoretical reason alone, substantial conclusions regarding: a) the soul or thinking subject (in the Paralogisms); b) the spatio-temporal world taken as whole including its relationship to freedom of the will (in the Antinomy of Pure Reason); and c) God (in the Ideal of Pure Reason).

# The Paralogisms of Pure Reason

*(A 341/B 399–A 405/B 432)*
Kant calls a metaphysician who attempts to prove the immortality of the soul a 'rational psychologist'. He does so in order to emphasize that unlike an empirical psychologist (who is interested in the *contents* of our thought), the metaphysician bases his proofs solely on the fact that every thought, whatever its content, is invariably referred by us to a self-conscious subject: the thinking subject or *I*. And the metaphysician attempts to reach certain conclusions about this thinking subject, this self-conscious subject of thought, which go beyond anything that sense experience can establish, but which, he believes, can be proved on the basis of rational argument.

The rational psychologist makes four key claims in respect to the soul or thinking subject. He claims first that the soul is a *substance* or *self-subsisting entity* (and so is not a mere *property* of some other thing); second, that the soul is a *simple* substance (and so cannot be divided or broken down into parts); third, that the soul is a substance that has a *continuous* existence; and fourth, that the soul's existence is *independent of all matter*. If these four claims can be proved by pure (theoretical) reason then the rational psychologist will have established the immortality of the soul, as this claim is normally understood. Since if the soul or *I* (the thinking subject) can be shown to be a substance that cannot be broken up and whose continuous existence is not dependent on anything material, it follows that the soul cannot cease to exist merely because the body dissolves at death. (As Kant points out, even if the soul were a simple substance, and so could not be destroyed by division, it might still – should it be dependent on the body – cease to exist by means of the gradual cessation of all its powers as the body dissolves at death, see B 413–15.)

But how is the rational psychologist to establish any of these claims? None of them can be established on the basis of our sense experience, i.e. on the basis of the perceptual evidence we can obtain during this bodily life. For no such sensible evidence could prove that the thinking subject cannot be broken up at the dissolution of the body or that its continuation is not dependent on the existence of the body. In order for these claims to be established, we need to know what happens following bodily death – and, hence, no sense experience during this life could prove that the soul survives the dissolution of the body.

This leaves the rational psychologist with the alternative of trying to prove his claims by means of pure (theoretical) reason. And this is, indeed, how he attempts to prove them. But, Kant argues, all of the rational psychologist's attempted proofs are fallacious (or paralogisms). At crucial points, they confuse *analytic* propositions – these tell us nothing about the *objective reality* of the rational psychologist's concept of the soul, i.e. whether that concept refers to any actual object – with informative *synthetic* ones. These synthetic propositions (with which the analytic ones are confused) require us to have *intuition* of the soul or thinking subject – and this, Kant points out, we simply cannot have. Yet without this intuition, the objective reality of the rational psychologist's concept of the soul – that it is a substance that is simple and can continue to exist beyond this (bodily) life – cannot be established in the way that the rational psychologist had hoped.

I shall largely follow the B edition of Kant's discussion of the Four Paralogisms:

1. So far as concerns the claim that the soul or *I* is a substance, the rationalist believes that this can be established by pointing out (correctly) that I can never think of myself as a mere predicate of any of my own judgements. For in judging, I am always the subject who is thinking or making the judgement. As Kant puts it, 'I am the *determining* subject of that relation which constitutes the judgment' (B 407; italics original). I cannot, therefore, consider myself as a *mere* predicate of any of my own judgements. But this feature of my acts of judging tells me nothing whatever about whether I exist in my own right, i.e. as a self-subsisting being (or substance), rather than depending on something else for thought or consciousness. In order to know whether I am a self-subsisting being, I would need to have intuition *of* the thinking subject. But that intuition is not given to me; for, in the nature of the case, the thinking subject is that which *has* sensible intuitions or representations. I can never be the object of one of my own thoughts (the contents of which are constituted by sensible intuitions, whether pure or empirical), given that I must always be that which is conscious of these thoughts. Since nothing presented to me can provide me with an intuition of my own nature as the judging or thinking subject, I cannot

tell anything *about* this nature from the analytic proposition that the *I* who is judging or thinking any proposition must always be regarded as its subject and never as its mere predicate.

2. Similarly, it is an analytic judgement that the subject that thinks any proposition must be simple in the sense that a *plurality* of synchronic subjects cannot comprehend the whole thought, expressed by that proposition, if each of them is only conscious of a *part* of that thought. In other words, it is true, indeed analytically true, that the *thinking* of any given proposition requires *one* act of consciousness in which the whole content of that proposition is entertained. But it does not follow that *what* has this one act of consciousness (the thinking subject or *I*) must itself be a simple substance – any more than one sound must be dependent on a single instrument, and not a plurality of them, in order to exist. Without an intuition of the thinking subject, we cannot determine whether it is or is not a simple substance. Such an intuition is necessarily debarred to us, since nothing that is given in sensible intuition – the only type of intuition we possess – can reveal to us the character of what has these sensible intuitions.

3. Again, it is an analytic judgement that if I am conscious of a number of temporally distinct representations as mine then I must think of this whole series as having occurred to the *same* subject (myself). But, as Kant points out, 'this cannot ... signify the identity of the person, if by this is understood the consciousness of the identity of one's own subject, as a thinking being, in all change of its states' (B 408). For without any *intuition* of the nature of this subject, I have no means of telling whether this subject remains the *same* substance throughout the given manifold or is constituted by a *succession* of short-lived substances, each of which has passed on its own consciousness of the manifold, as well as that of its predecessors, to the next substance (see A 363–4). On the latter hypothesis, the subject would still have a consciousness, via memory, of all the earlier members of the manifold as ones of which it has been conscious, even though there would not be a *single* substance existing throughout that manifold. In short, I can tell nothing about the diachronic *nature* of the thinking subject – whether it is one continuously existing substance or made up of changing substances – from the analytic judgement that in order to be conscious of a

series of temporally distinct representations as mine, I must ascribe all the members of that series to the same subject (myself).

4. Finally, it is an analytic judgement that I can distinguish myself as a thinking being from other things outside me. For if I could not distinguish things outside me from myself as a thinking being, I could not think of them as *other* things. And I can certainly distinguish, in thought, between things that exist in space, including my own body, from what exists in time only (namely, my own acts of consciousness). But this tells me nothing about whether it would be so much as possible for consciousness of myself to continue *independent* of what is outside me. For, so far as I know, it is that which is outside me – including my own body – that makes possible all my acts of self-consciousness. I have no intuition by which I can tell whether, *without* what is outside me, consciousness of myself would still be possible and, hence, whether I could continue to exist as a thinking thing.

\*

Before we conclude this brief discussion of the Paralogisms, it is worth reviewing, in general terms, why the rational psychologist's arguments have failed. Take as an example his claim that the soul is simple. As Kant notes, the claim is a synthetic one, since no mere analysis of the concepts of *soul* and *simplicity* could prove (or disprove) it. At the same time, the claim cannot be proved by employing sense experience, as we have seen. Whether our soul or thinking subject will be dissolved at bodily death cannot be established on the basis of our sense experience (the sensible evidence we obtain during this bodily life). Yet the *raison d'être* for proving the simplicity of the soul is to show that it will not cease to exist with the dissolution of the body. So the claim that the soul is simple is a synthetic a priori judgement: it is a synthetic claim that can only be established, if it can be established at all, *independent of sense experience*. But – and this is the vital point – *unlike* the synthetic a priori judgements of pure mathematics and natural science, the synthetic a priori judgement that the soul is simple cannot be established by showing that it helps to make our sense experience possible. For in criticizing the rational psychologist's argument, Kant has shown that we cannot determine whether the thinking subject is or is not simple – and yet, either way, our capacity *in this life* to be conscious, and so to have sense experience, will be unaffected. Consequently, the judgement that the soul is simple completely *transcends* our sense experience. Not only is it impossible to prove the judgement *on the basis of* our sense experience, it is also impossible to prove it by showing that *it makes this experience possible*. But if it cannot be shown to make our sense experience possible, it follows that, since it is not analytic, it cannot be proved by means of pure (theoretical) reason. This important conclusion, remember, is one that Kant has already drawn from his investigations into the possibility of pure mathematics and natural science. These investigations have shown that the only way in which pure (theoretical) reason can establish any synthetic a priori judgement is by showing that it *makes sense experience possible*. If such a judgement cannot be established in this way, it cannot be proved *or* disproved by pure (theoretical) reason. For unless our thought has some sensible intuition upon which to exercise itself, its a priori concepts (the categories) have nothing with which to engage, and our judgements will be empty of theoretical content. Since metaphysics is, for Kant, a discipline which must establish its claims on the basis of pure (theoretical) reason *alone*, it follows that metaphysics is unable to prove or disprove that the soul is simple.

Analogous considerations apply in the other two main sections of the Dialectic, the Antinomy and the Ideal of Pure Reason. In both, Kant will argue that once transcendental idealism is accepted, it can be seen that the synthetic a priori judgements in these two fields can contribute nothing to making our sense experience possible; in fact, they completely transcend sense experience. As a result, pure (theoretical) reason is unable to determine their truth value. Metaphysics, therefore, should abandon its attempt to establish any conclusions in these fields, just as it should with regard to our soul or thinking subject.

# The Antinomy of Pure Reason

*(A 405/B 432–A 567/B 595)*
Whereas, in the Paralogisms and the Ideal of Pure Reason, Kant is concerned to unmask the errors committed by metaphysicians in

their attempts respectively to prove the immortality of the soul and the existence of God, in the Antinomies, he is concerned to do rather more than show why we should reject the attempts by metaphysicians to prove or disprove certain synthetic a priori judgements (here, about the spatio-temporal world taken as a whole). He is, at the same time, seeking to convince us that transcendental realism cannot conceivably be the correct theory of our relationship to the spatio-temporal world. As we have noted, the transcendental realist holds that the objects of the senses exist in space and/or time, quite independently of our capacity to perceive them: in other words, the transcendental realist holds that spatio-temporal objects (the objects of our senses) are things in themselves.

Of course, Kant believes that he has already shown that transcendental realism must be rejected by means of his arguments in the Transcendental Aesthetic: he believes that he has established there that space and time are properties of our mind alone (they are to be identified with our forms of outer and inner intuition respectively), and that spatio-temporal objects are, accordingly, merely appearances (as such they possess no existence other than as actual or possible items of our consciousness). These are key claims of his alternative theory, transcendental idealism. But, in the Antinomy of Pure Reason, Kant proposes a *further* argument against transcendental realism and in favour of transcendental idealism. This argument is that if transcendental realism is accepted then we shall find ourselves involved in inevitable *contradictions*, whereas if we embrace transcendental idealism, these contradictions *disappear* (and no new ones are discovered in their place). Consequently, on the assumption that these two theories exhaustively delineate our possible relationship to the objects of the senses (and Kant does make this – not unreasonable – assumption), it follows that a proof of the impossibility of transcendental realism is, at the same time, a proof of the correctness of transcendental idealism.

There are four Antinomies. These are divided into two pairs: the first pair are termed 'Mathematical Antinomies' and the second pair 'Dynamical Antinomies'. The Mathematical Antinomies are so-called because each is concerned with the *extent* of a series existing in the spatio-temporal world (here the members of the series must all be of the same type in order to form part of one series). The Dynamical Antinomies are so-called because each is concerned with the *cause* of a given series existing in the spatio-temporal world (here there is no requirement that the cause need be similar in nature to the members of the series, since it is allowed that, in general, something can be a cause without requiring that it be of the same nature as its effect). In the case of each of the four Antinomies, there is a thesis and an antithesis. A metaphysician who, with respect to a given Antinomy, propounds the thesis is called a 'dogmatist' and, analogously, a metaphysician who propounds the antithesis is called an 'empiricist'. As each pair of thesis and antithesis is argued for by these metaphysicians, they really do (Kant believes) contradict one other. He will show why this is so. He will also explain how, in each case, the contradiction can be avoided.

I shall not discuss in detail all four Antinomies, but only one Mathematical and one Dynamical Antinomy. Both Mathematical Antinomies receive similar, though not identical, treatment; and so I hope that a discussion of one of them, the First Antinomy – which is concerned with the age and size of the world – will also sufficiently serve to illustrate Kant's general strategy for the Second Antinomy. In the case of the Dynamical Antinomies, I shall discuss the Third Antinomy – which is concerned with freedom – both because it is the most important of all the Antinomies and because Kant discusses the significant issues raised by the Fourth Antinomy more fully in the Ideal of Pure Reason.

## Mathematical Antinomies (First and Second Antinomies)

First Antinomy:
*Thesis*: The world has a beginning in time and is enclosed within boundaries in space.
*Antithesis*: The world is, as to time and space, infinite.

Second Antinomy:
*Thesis*: Everything in the world is constituted out of the simple.
*Antithesis*: There is nothing simple in the world, but everything is composite.

In the case of each of these two Antinomies, Kant contends that *both* the thesis (attributed to the dogmatist) *and* the antithesis (attributed to the empiricist) are *false* because although, in every case, a formally valid argument is presented, each argument rests on the same mistaken presupposition. This common presupposition is that the objects of the senses are spatio-temporal objects *conceived as things in themselves*. Once this presupposition is dropped, and replaced with the view that spatio-temporal objects are merely constituted by mind-dependent phenomena (representations), it can be shown that the thesis and the antithesis of both Mathematical Antinomies are false. As Kant sees it, once we embrace transcendental idealism, there are no contradictions in our thinking about the age and size of the spatio-temporal world, or about the composition of what exists in this world – as there undoubtedly are contradictions (and with both Mathematical Antinomies), if we adopt the common presupposition of the dogmatist and empiricist, viz. transcendental realism.

*

Let us now look at the grounds that are offered for the thesis and antithesis of the first of the two Mathematical Antinomies. The thesis asserts that the world has a beginning in time and is bounded or limited in space. According to the dogmatist, this (dual) claim can be proved by showing that if it were *not* true – which the dogmatist takes as equivalent to holding that the world does not have a beginning in time 'but has existed from all eternity' and is infinitely extended in space – we would necessarily involve ourselves in absurdity. As regards time, the dogmatist argues that on the supposition that the world had no beginning in time, this must imply that, up until the present moment, an infinite number of successive states of the world must have passed away. But this is impossible because our notion of *infinity* entails that an infinite number of states can never be completed by successive enumeration. Hence, the series of successive states leading up to the present existence of the world can never be completed on the supposition that the world has existed from eternity. Yet it is plain that the world does now exist. Therefore, the world must have a beginning in time. As regards space, the dogmatist argues that if the world could be conceived as infinitely extended in space, we must be able to think of this infinite extension as capable of being completed by successive addition of its parts (since it is impossible for an infinite extension of coexisting states of the world to be given in any single intuition). But, assuming the extension of the world is infinite, the successive addition of its parts can never be completed. Hence, it must be impossible to think of the world as infinitely extended in space and, consequently, the alleged concept of a world infinitely extended in space must be rejected as incoherent. Therefore the world must be bounded or limited in space.

The antithesis asserts that the world has no beginning in time and is infinitely extended in space. In order to establish this claim, the empiricist asks us to assume that it is *not* true – which the empiricist takes as equivalent to holding that the world does have a beginning in time and is bounded or limited in space. As regards time, the empiricist argues that, on the assumption that the world does have beginning, it must be possible to assign a point *within* the temporal continuum at which the world began. But since there is nothing preceding the beginning of the world – *ex hypothesi*, the temporal continuum is otherwise empty – it is impossible to assign, within this continuum, any point at which the world could have begun. Therefore, the world can have no beginning in time. As regards space, the empiricist argues that, on the supposition that the world is bounded or limited in space, it must be possible in principle to identify where the boundary points or limits of the world lie. But since there is nothing outside the world – *ex hypothesi*, space is otherwise empty – it is impossible to conceive of the world as bounded or limited in space. A boundary or limit to something is only conceivable if there is some other thing outside or beyond it *in relation to which* that something is bounded. But there is nothing beyond the world, since empty space is not a substance but what makes the existence of substances possible. Hence, it is impossible to conceive of a boundary or limit to the world. Therefore, the world must be infinitely extended in space.

These, then, are the thesis and antithesis of the First Antinomy, together with a summary of the arguments in their favour. To repeat, Kant takes these arguments to be valid; that is, he regards both the thesis and antithesis as genuinely following from their respective premises. Accordingly, granting the premises, there must be a straight contradiction in our thinking both about the age and the size of the whole world (or cosmos): we are committed to thinking both that the world has a beginning in time and that it has existed from all eternity, and we are also committed to thinking both that the world is finitely extended in space and that it is infinitely extended in space.

As it stands, we are in a mess. Kant points out that all these arguments assume that the world which we experience is constituted by things in themselves existing in space and time. For both the dogmatist and the empiricist accept that although we cannot prove by means of our senses that the world has either a finite or an infinite age and, likewise, that it has either a finite or infinite spatial extent, there is nonetheless, in each case, a truth of the matter which reason can establish. The trouble is that, on the assumption that the world of the senses exists in itself, reason is genuinely able to prove (as Kant holds) the finite and infinite age of the world as well as the finite and infinite spatial extension of the world.

But what happens if we *drop* the assumption that spatio-temporal objects are things in themselves, and hold, instead, that they are merely constituted by representations in our sensible forms of intuition? In that case, Kant claims, we can show that *both* the thesis *and* the antithesis are false: the world has neither a finite age and a finite spatial extension nor an infinite age and an infinite spatial extension. For if spatio-temporal objects are merely constituted by our representations, it follows that they exist only as possible objects of our perceptual consciousness (unlike things in themselves, they can have no existence independent of us). It therefore becomes impossible for reason to reach any definite conclusion concerning the age and size of the whole world. Once spatio-temporal objects are taken to be merely mind-dependent phenomena (representations), we cannot declare the world to have a beginning in time or to have existed from all eternity, and we cannot declare that it is finitely or infinitely extended in space. All we can say is that it is known to exist as far back in time and as far out in space as our perceptions have so far reached. But we can set no determinate limit (finite or infinite) to either its age or size precisely because the spatio-temporal world exists only in and through the successive series of our possible perceptions. No perception can ever be experienced as terminating the series (hence the phenomenal series cannot be taken as finite). Equally, there can be no conceivable warrant for claiming that the possible series of perceptions must be infinite in number (hence the series cannot be taken as infinite). An assertion of either the finite or infinite extent of our perceptions could only be taken as correct if the world of our perceptions existed *in itself* (for

only then could the series of our perceptions be finite or infinite).
Kant sums up his own position thus:

> This ... series can, therefore, be neither greater nor smaller than
> the possible empirical regress upon which alone its concept rests.
> And since this regress can yield neither a determinate infinite nor
> a determinate finite (that is, anything absolutely limited), it is
> evident that the magnitude of the world can be taken neither as
> finite nor as infinite. The regress, through which it is represented,
> allows of neither alternative.
>
> *(A 519/B 547 [footnote])*

## Criticism of the Mathematical Antinomies

I will not take up the various criticisms of Kant's claim that his stated
arguments for the dogmatist theses and the empiricist antitheses are
all valid. (For the most part, the force of these criticisms hinges on
whether Kant has a correct concept of *the mathematically infinite*.
Clearly, if he does not, this will put in jeopardy his claim that the
dogmatist and empiricist arguments are, without exception, valid.)
Rather, the criticism I shall consider alleges that, even if Kant's
own versions of these arguments are all formally valid, he cannot
possibly use this fact to his own advantage. And the reason is that he
is accused of *assuming* his own theory, transcendental idealism, in
stating the arguments of both the dogmatist theses and the empiricist
antitheses. If this criticism is right, it must represent a serious attack
on his strategy in the Mathematical Antinomies. Kant is trying to
convince us that transcendental idealism is the correct theory of our
relationship to the objects of our hoped-for perceptual knowledge
by showing that the *alternative* theory, transcendental realism,
leads to contradictions. But if e.g. the argument for the dogmatist
thesis of the First Antinomy employs transcendental idealism (and
not transcendental realism) in demonstrating the impossibility of
the empiricist antithesis (equally for the empiricist's argument), it
would clearly be unacceptable to maintain that it is the assumption
of *transcendental realism* which is leading the dogmatist and the
empiricist into inevitable conflict with each other.

I believe, however, that this criticism is unfounded. I shall illustrate why this is so by reference to the First Antinomy (here the issue

is more straightforward than in the Second Antinomy). At no place in the stated argument of either the thesis or antithesis of the First Antinomy do the rival parties hold that their opponent's position is false *because* the world of our senses exists only as constituted by representations. Rather, each of the arguments assumes that the world which we know by means of our senses (the spatio-temporal world) exists in itself, and the opposing position is rejected because that position requires something which we cannot *think* or *conceive* concerning the world's age or size. Both the dogmatist and empiricist accept that no possible perception(s) could settle the question of the age or size of the world. But since, according to them, the spatio-temporal world exists in itself – and so *independent* of our possible perceptions – the issue is not thereby settled. It is not settled because, if the world exists in itself, it must be true that both the age and size of the world *are* determinate, despite the impossibility of deciding the matter by reference to our perceptions. And, as Kant sees it, both the dogmatist and empiricist do each have a valid a priori proof demonstrating the impossibility of their opponent's claim concerning the age and size of the world. I hope my summary of their arguments above has shown that, according to each party, their opponent's position must be rejected because it is not even a *thinkable* position: it is not rejected because, although it is admitted to be thinkable, we will never be in a position to *discover* its truth by means of our possible perceptions.

I conclude that Kant's belief that – at least – the First Mathematical Antinomy, together with his solution of it, constitutes a new and decisive reason for accepting transcendental idealism (and rejecting transcendental realism) should not be dismissed on the supposed grounds that the arguments he provides for the dogmatist thesis and the empiricist antithesis take for granted the very position he is trying to justify.

# Dynamical Antinomies (Third and Fourth Antinomies)

Third Antinomy:
*Thesis*: There are in the world causes through freedom.
*Antithesis*: Everything in the world happens solely in accordance with laws of nature.

Fourth Antinomy:
*Thesis*: In the series of world-causes there is some necessary being.
*Antithesis*: There is nothing necessary in the world, but in this series all is contingent.

As with the Mathematical Antinomies, Kant holds that the arguments put forward by the dogmatist and the empiricist respectively do validly imply the theses and antitheses of the Dynamical Antinomies. Accordingly, the thesis and antithesis of both the Third and Fourth Antinomies are also really in conflict on the assumption of transcendental realism. But, *unlike* the Mathematical Antinomies, Kant does not think that his resolution of this second pair of antinomies implies the falsity of both their theses and antitheses. Instead, he thinks that if we adopt transcendental idealism, we can say that both the theses and the antitheses of the two Dynamical Antinomies *may* be true. In fact, the truth of both the dynamical antitheses is accepted throughout (though not as these antitheses are understood by the empiricist): the challenge is to show that, given transcendental idealism, accepting these antitheses is compatible with at least the logical possibility of the dynamical theses *also* being true. For example, Kant certainly accepts the antithesis of the Third Antinomy, viz. that every event happens solely in accordance with the laws of nature. The issue is whether, within Kant's *own* system, the acceptance of this claim can be rendered consistent with the possibility of the thesis also being true, namely that causality through freedom exists.

Note that if the Dynamical Antinomies are truly in conflict assuming transcendental realism, while the conflicts disappear assuming transcendental idealism, then this will provide grounds, independent of any offered in the Aesthetic, for accepting the latter theory and rejecting the former. Moreover, since Kant's method for defusing the conflicts arising in the Dynamical Antinomies is rather different from the method he adopts in the Mathematical Antinomies, his treatment of the Dynamical Antinomies could provide this independent ground even if his treatment of both of the Mathematical Antinomies should fail to do so (or vice versa).

As I said earlier, I shall not discuss both Dynamical Antinomies but only the Third Antinomy. Kant's treatment of it, and more particularly his proposed solution of the conflict between the thesis and antithesis, is of pivotal importance to his moral philosophy. It is the proposed solution which will largely occupy us.

## Third Antinomy and Kant's resolution

The dogmatist supports the thesis of the Third Antinomy by arguing that if we suppose that causality in accordance with the laws of nature is the *only* form of causality, we could never provide a complete explanation for any event. We could not because, on the supposition, the cause of an event would *itself* require an explanation of its occurrence, i.e. a cause of its action, and this earlier cause would again require a still earlier cause and so on. But the laws of nature affirm that everything takes place according to a cause which is itself *sufficiently* determined. Hence, the claim that causality is only possible in accordance with the laws of nature is a self-contradictory one (since no cause could be sufficiently determined). The dogmatist concludes that there must be *another* type of cause acting in the world, viz. a cause that does not itself require any antecedent cause of its action. Such a cause would possess *absolute spontaneity* 'whereby a series of appearances, which proceeds in accordance with the laws of nature, begins *of itself*' (A 446/B 474; italics original). Any cause which acts in this way exhibits what Kant calls 'transcendental freedom'.

The empiricist supports the antithesis by arguing that if we suppose that transcendental freedom exists in the world of our experience, it would follow that some causes act in this world without any antecedent cause of their coming to be, i.e. they would possess absolute spontaneity. Such a supposition would destroy our capacity to distinguish hallucinatory or delusory occurrences from veridical experiences, since this capacity relies on every possible (veridical) experience being subject to the laws of nature. Now the dogmatist accepts that we do experience objects and events in the world. Hence, everything that happens in the world, so far as it can be experienced, must be completely subject to the laws of nature.

That, in outline, is Kant's exposition of the dogmatist and empiricist arguments for the thesis and antithesis of the Third Antinomy. Since he regards their conflict as unavoidable, given transcendental realism, he concludes that this theory cannot correctly expound the relationship between ourselves and spatio-temporal objects.

*

Of greater interest is the question of how Kant is going to resolve the conflict on his *own* theory, transcendental idealism. This is a pressing question for him because he has argued, in the Second Analogy, that everything that happens must have a cause in the spatio-temporal world, i.e. a natural cause. On the face of it, therefore, there would seem to be no place for transcendental freedom on the transcendental idealist's theory. Yet it is essential that transcendental freedom is not completely ruled out because Kant claims that we can only be morally praised or blamed for anything we do in so far as we are capable of making and acting upon transcendentally free decisions. However, since every action – as an event in the spatio-temporal world – must have a natural cause which itself has a natural cause and so on indefinitely, how is it even logically possible for any of our actions to result from transcendentally free decisions? Unless Kant can defend at least the logical possibility of transcendental freedom in the face of (what he himself accepts as) the thoroughgoing natural determinism in the spatio-temporal world, his moral philosophy will be in ruins.

In his attempt to resolve the ostensible conflict between the requirement that everything that happens must have a natural cause and the possibility of human agents exercising transcendental freedom, Kant wheels in his distinction between the world of appearances (the phenomenal world) and the world of things in themselves (the noumenal or intelligible world). He fully acknowledges that when we consider ourselves merely as appearances, as beings existing in nature, every one of our actions, like every other event in the spatio-temporal world, must be capable of falling under the law of natural causality. Accordingly, from the perspective of the world of appearances alone, human agents cannot be regarded as free since all their actions must result from natural causes (which themselves have natural causes and so on). However, we can *also* consider ourselves as beings that have an existence as things in themselves. Considered from *this* perspective, we exist outside space and time, and so, in respect of the use of those of our faculties that form part of our existence as things in themselves, we are not governed by any of the laws of nature (since these laws only apply in the spatio-temporal world). Kant holds that our faculties of understanding and reason – our intellectual faculties – must be regarded as belonging to us as things in themselves. They must, he thinks, because these faculties are concerned only with the *form*, never with the *content*, of any data; and, as such, they must operate *independently* of the influence from any appearance, from anything empirical. Consequently, as subjects existing in the noumenal world, we can make decisions – by exercising our purely intellectual faculty of reason – that are transcendentally free. So, the argument concludes, it is possible to regard ourselves, qua noumenal subjects, as capable of acting in the world of appearances on transcendentally free decisions, despite the fact that when we consider ourselves *merely* as phenomenal subjects (as beings existing in the world of appearances), every one of our actions must be regarded as wholly resulting from natural causes.

## Criticism of Kant's resolution

This (briefly stated) defence of transcendental freedom is open to a number of objections. Much the most serious seems to me to be this. Even if we allow that it is logically possible that the world *as a whole* could have a transcendentally free cause – a first cause – there can be no room for such freedom with respect to anything that exists *within* the world. And this restriction must certainly apply to us, considered as active rational beings or agents. Let it be granted (following Kant) that we can think of ourselves as subjects that have an existence in the noumenal world as well as in the world of appearances, and that, as noumenal subjects, we can make transcendentally free *decisions*. Nonetheless – the objection continues – it is plain that we cannot translate these decisions into *actions* which can make any difference to what happens in the spatio-temporal world. Consider a case where an agent knowingly does something that is morally wrong as a result of a naturally produced desire. How can we say that the agent *ought not* to have performed that action? The agent's natural desire (which *ex hypothesi* caused the action) has itself a prior natural cause and so on indefinitely back in time. Accordingly, no decision by the noumenal subject to act otherwise, in the circumstances in which the agent acted, could have been translated into action. It could not since the action that actually occurs has *already* been naturally determined by an earlier series of events in the spatio-temporal world (by the occurrence of the agent's natural desire, which itself has a prior natural cause and so on). Kant's defence of our capacity to act morally through transcendental freedom is, therefore, manifestly in conflict with his requirement that everything that happens must have a natural cause. Far from resolving the antinomy, Kant has made it *logically impossible* for transcendentally free actions ever to occur on his own theory, transcendental idealism.

In my view, Kant's response to this objection provides the best way of grasping the main strands of his whole defence of transcendental freedom as applied to human agents. Following Hume, he thinks of an agent's actions as arising from a combination of two factors: on the one hand, the agent's character and, on the other, the circumstances in which the agent believes himself to be placed. Both philosophers think of an agent's character as comprising a set of personality traits or dispositions to act (in the *Critique of Pure Reason*, this character is described as the agent's 'empirical character'). For example, to describe someone as 'mendacious' (a personality trait) is to maintain that the agent will be disposed to act in an untruthful way under certain circumstances; and to describe someone as 'kind-hearted' is to maintain that the agent will be disposed to act in kindly ways under certain circumstances. We explain why agents have acted or will act in a given way by reference to one or more of their personality traits, together with the circumstances in which they think of themselves as placed.

How does Kant (and Hume) suppose that we are able to credit personality traits to agents in the first place? By observing how they have acted, under different circumstances, in the past. Once we are familiar with a particular agent's individual character – by means of our observations of that agent's past behaviour and our knowledge of human nature in general (also gleaned from observation) – we can go on to predict or explain further actions of that agent. Although vastly more complex, Kant thinks of the way in which we seek to provide explanations or predictions of human actions as no different, in principle, from the everyday way in which we provide explanations or predictions for the behaviour of e.g. a squash ball when it strikes a wall of the court. On the assumption, then, that we really can explain or predict the actions of human agents by reference to their empirical characters and perceived circumstances – and Kant, following Hume, does make this assumption – we shall have provided a wholly naturalistic causal account of their behaviour: an account that is fully in accord with Kant's demand that everything that happens in the world of appearances must be subject to the law of natural causality (the principle of sufficient reason).

Now the question is this. Is it possible to think of the noumenal subject as responsible for an agent's actions granting this naturalistic causal model? Kant believes that it is, because we can view the noumenal subject as responsible for every one of the personality traits – and so *the entire empirical character* – of the agent. His idea is that while we are born with, and perhaps further acquire, naturally determined drives – which, under given circumstances, manifest themselves as sensuous desires to act in certain ways – it is not inevitable that these felt drives are actually *operative*, that is, are translated into *actions*. Some will and some will not be *depending on the noumenal subject*. Certainly, where, for any particular agent, a given drive does lead to action on *one* occasion, the same action by that agent must *always* follow under the same circumstances (given the thoroughgoing determinism in the spatio-temporal world). But that in no way interferes with the freedom of the noumenal subject. This subject decides whether, under the given circumstances, to act on the basis of reason alone (and so to act morally) or to allow the naturally produced desire to be operative (and so to bring about an action that has no positive moral worth). Yet, whichever type of action appears, the noumenal subject cannot have been determined in its choice by the law of natural causality, since that law only applies to what exists within the spatio-temporal framework. Further, as an atemporal entity, its choice of action, under the given circumstances, is not subject to change; and so this choice will express itself, in the world of appearances, in an entirely regular way (under the same circumstances).

It is our observation of the agent's various modes of behaviour, as these are manifested under different circumstances, which enables us to ascribe a set of personality traits, a particular empirical character, to an agent; and from that we are able to explain or predict further actions in accordance with the law of natural causality. Of course, the noumenal subject has only *exercised* transcendental freedom where actions of genuine moral worth appear in the spatio-temporal world. But, in every case of acknowledged moral import, the agent, qua noumenal subject, can be held responsible – even for those actions that are produced by sensuous desires – because nothing in the temporal series of events can have determined the noumenal subject to create the particular empirical character that is expressed through the agent's actions, i.e. as these appear in the spatio-temporal world.

How, then, will Kant respond to the criticism raised above, namely, that if an agent acts immorally on the basis of a naturally produced desire, it is impossible for any decision of the noumenal subject to have prevented that action? His response will be that we can regard the noumenal subject as choosing to allow the naturally produced desire to be *operative*. Although it is not within the power of the noumenal self to control whether a particular type of sensuous desire occurs (that depends on the set of natural drives that one happens to possess as well as the circumstances in which one finds oneself), we can still think that it is up to the noumenal subject whether the naturally determined desire leads to *action* under those circumstances. For it is not a consequence of Kant's demand that every event must have a natural cause that the agent should ever act on any particular type and strength of sensuous desire. Undoubtedly, whether or not any given sensuous desire leads to action, it will have a natural cause of its coming to be felt (whenever it is felt), and this cause, in turn, will have had a still earlier natural cause of its occurrence and so on. But that is irrelevant to the question of whether this naturally produced desire could have been prevented from bringing about the ensuing action. On Kant's distinction between the world of appearances and the world of things in themselves, it is not self-contradictory to hold that the naturally produced desire need not have brought about the action, viz. if the noumenal subject had exercised its transcendental freedom and acted through reason alone (thereby preventing this particular felt desire from ever being operative under the given type of circumstances). If such a choice had been made, this would have expressed itself in similar moral actions always being performed by the agent, under the same circumstances. As a result, the empirical character of the agent would have been correspondingly *different*. Accordingly, even if the agent had acted through reason alone, there would have been no break in the law of natural causality, whereby we explain an agent's actions on the basis of character traits and perceived circumstances. At the same time, we can rightly

blame the agent for acting immorally, under the given circumstances, since nothing in the series of natural events leading up to
that action could have prevented the agent, qua noumenal subject,
from exercising its transcendental freedom and acting morally.

*

In outlining Kant's defence of transcendental freedom in the face
of the thoroughgoing determinism of the spatio-temporal world,
I have, following his own discussion of the Third Antinomy, only
been concerned to show that the existence of transcendental
freedom is *logically possible*, assuming transcendental idealism
(but not transcendental realism). In the *Critique of Pure Reason*
that is the most that he tries to do. In his moral writings, and
most especially in the *Critique of Practical Reason*, he seeks to go
further and prove the *reality* of transcendental freedom, i.e. that
such freedom does actually exist, given transcendental idealism.
We shall investigate this attempted proof, together with the related
ones concerning the existence of God and the immortality of the
soul, when we discuss Kant's moral philosophy.

# The Ideal of Pure Reason

*(A 567/B 595–A 642/B 670)*
Kant maintains that there can be only three attempted proofs of
God's existence based on pure (theoretical) reason. Collectively,
he calls these 'the speculative proofs'. His ground for claiming
that there can only be three is that he believes that any speculative
argument for God's existence must take one of three possible
forms. First, the argument could be wholly independent of any
experience, and so based on a priori concepts and premises alone.
Second, it could be an argument which relies on the fact of some
experience or other, without worrying about the content of that
experience. Third, the argument could be based on our actual
detailed observations of nature. The first type of argument he calls
'ontological', the second 'cosmological' and the third 'physico-
theological' (more familiarly called 'the argument from design').
Kant rejects all three argument types and, consequently, the entire
enterprise of attempting to prove God's existence on the basis of
pure (theoretical) reason.

# The Ontological Argument

(A 592/B 620–A 602/631)

Advocates of the Ontological Argument claim that the supreme being (or *ens realissimum*) – that which has all positive properties or attributes to the highest degree – can be shown to have an absolutely necessary existence. Kant has two related lines of attack against the argument.

The first line of attack urges that it is simply unclear what can even be meant by talking of an *object* having an absolutely or unconditionally necessary existence or, equivalently, an *object* whose non-existence is impossible. The standard explanation is to compare it with examples, generally from mathematics, in which – it is alleged – necessity is applied, and perfectly intelligibly applied, to an object. For instance, we can say that a triangle necessarily has three sides (or, alternatively, that it is impossible for anything to be a triangle and not to have three sides). But, as Kant points out, such examples are not analogous to the alleged case of an object having an absolutely necessary existence. For the examples offered are of the unconditional necessity of a judgement *about* an object; they are not cases where an object is *itself* claimed to be unconditionally necessary. On the contrary, when it is said that 'it is absolutely or unconditionally necessary that a triangle has three sides', this does not affirm either that a triangle or three sides are absolutely necessary; it only affirms that *if* there is a triangle, three sides will necessarily be found in it. Such claims, in other words, only affirm conditional, not unconditional, necessity of the object or of what is predicated of it. Accordingly, while it is indeed self-contradictory to affirm the existence of an object answering to the concept of a triangle and yet reject its having three sides, there is no contradiction in denying the existence of any object answering to that concept (and, hence, any object having three sides).

Kant plausibly holds that it is merely a confusion to suppose that the alleged absolute or unconditional necessity of an object existing can be understood in the same way as we understand a judgement about e.g. the necessity of a triangle existing with three sides. For the way in which we understand the mathematical judgement *does* make it possible to deny the necessity of a triangle existing or, equivalently, of three sides existing. And since the only way in which it has been explained how talk of 'necessity' can be understood, with reference to an object, is within a judgement about the object (where the reference is to conditional, not unconditional, necessity of the object and its properties), Kant concludes that no sense has been attached to the alleged concept of *an absolutely necessary being*.

Despite these criticisms, he acknowledges that proponents of the Ontological Argument believe that there is just *one* concept where the rejection of the object's existence is self-contradictory, where its non-existence is impossible. This is the concept of a being that has all positive attributes to the highest degree, the *ens realissimum*. Kant's second line of attack is directed specifically against those proponents of the Ontological Argument who believe that this concept, and this concept alone, avoids his general objections to the cogency of any object possessing absolutely necessary existence.

The proponents maintain that since the concept of the *ens realissimum* is a possible one, it follows that such a being must exist. For (they argue) it would be self-contradictory to acknowledge that a concept, which is a possible one, should contain all reality and yet deny that its object exists. It would be self-contradictory because 'existence' must be included in 'all reality'. Kant's well-known criticism of this argument hinges on his claim that 'existence' does not refer to any property, any characteristic, of an object, although it is here being treated as if it does. We cannot argue that because the concept of the *ens realissimum* is a logically possible one – and, hence, can be *thought* without contradiction – it follows that the object of this concept must exist. For if that were a valid inference, it would mean that in thinking about the object in accordance with its concept, our thought would leave out one of the properties of the object, namely its existence. It would mean that we could never have a thought about the object which fully characterizes the object, since we would always be omitting one of the properties of the object itself:

> [B]y however many predicates we may think a thing – even if we completely determine it – we do not make the least addition to the thing when we further declare that this thing *is*. Otherwise, it would not be exactly the same thing that exists, but something more than we had thought in the concept; and we could not then say that the exact object of my concept exists. If we think

in a thing every feature of reality except one, the missing reality is not added by my saying that this defective thing exists. On the contrary, it exists with the same defect with which I have thought it, since otherwise what exists would be something different from what I thought.

*(A 600/B 628)*

Accordingly, when it is asked what properties something must have in order to satisfy the concept of the *ens realissimum*, the answer cannot include 'existence' (as it might include 'omnipotence') because 'existence' is not a real predicate, i.e. it does not refer to a property, or characteristic, of an object. It serves rather to indicate, truly or falsely, that there is an object which answers to the given concept. Hence, it is fallacious to move from the logical possibility of the concept of the *ens realissimum* to its necessary existence on the grounds that to deny the existence of this object would be self-contradictory.

# The Cosmological Argument

*(A 603/B 631–A 614/B 642)*
This speculative argument seeks to prove the existence of God – a being having all positive attributes to the highest possible degree (the *ens realissimum*) – from the mere fact of experience, even if that experience should be only the consciousness of one's own existence. No account is taken of the particular *content* of any possible experience. Kant sets out the argument in this way:

> If anything exists, an absolutely necessary being must also exist. Now I, at least exist. Therefore an absolutely necessary being exists ... The necessary being can be determined in one way only, that is, by one out of each pair of possible predicates. It must therefore be *completely* determined through its own concept. Now there is only one possible concept which determines a thing completely a priori, namely, the concept of the *ens realissimum*. The concept of the *ens realissimum* is therefore the only concept through which a necessary being can be thought. In other words, a supreme being necessarily exists.
>
> *(A 604/B 632–A 607/B 635; italics original)*

Unsurprisingly, Kant objects to this argument on the grounds that no good reason has been offered for why the existence of a series of causes and effects – starting from the consciousness of one's own existence – must terminate with a first cause, with something that cannot be dependent for its existence on anything else: 'an absolutely necessary being' as the argument puts it. We certainly cannot assume such a terminus *within* experience – both the Second Analogy and the resolution of the First Antinomy have made that clear – and we have no grounds for holding that, *outside* experience, it is impossible for there to be an infinite series of causes and effects. Once we pass beyond experience, we can have no grounds for either affirming or denying the existence of any cause or series of causes. In fact, Kant contends that even the *claim* that there must be a cause beyond our possible experience has not been given any determinate meaning. For, as the Analytic has argued, we can only grasp what it could mean for something to count as a *cause* within possible experience. If we *remove* reference to any possible experience, and nevertheless seek to establish a cause of what exists within the world, we have no criterion by which to grasp what could answer to this pure concept.

However, Kant devotes most of his critical attention not to the objection above (this is passed over very rapidly), but to his further claim that the cosmological argument could only go through if the ontological argument were valid. He thinks that the cosmological argument has to rely on the ontological argument because even if we allow the proof of an absolutely necessary being as the ground upon which our experience must depend (which, as we have just seen, he does not think that we should allow), there is no hope of identifying this necessary being with the *ens realissimum* without relying on the ontological argument.

His reasons for making the claim that the cosmological argument depends on the ontological argument are tortuous, and have led a number of commentators to dismiss the claim as unsubstantiated. But I think Kant's essential point against the speculative metaphysician is that the latter has to employ the following line of argument in order to prove that the *ens realissimum* is identical with the absolutely necessary being: 'The only way in which, by means of theoretical reason, we can conceive something as an absolutely necessary being is by thinking of its existence as included in its essence. For *ex hypothesi* the absolutely necessary being cannot be dependent for its existence on anything else:

if it were, it could not be an absolutely necessary being, i.e. a being that can depend on no other condition whatsoever in order to exist. But the only way in which theoretical reason can recognize a thing's existence as unconditionally necessary – and so as absolutely necessary – is if its existence is contained in its essence. Unless existence is included in its essence, its existence can still be conceived as dependent on something else and, hence, it cannot, at the same time, be recognized as unconditionally necessary. Now the ontological argument has shown that there is one, and only one, concept from which a being's existence can be recognized by theoretical reason as unconditionally necessary, i.e. as included in its essence, and that is the concept of the *ens realissimum*. Consequently, the *ens realissimum* is the only concept which theoretical reason can think of as an absolutely necessary being.'

Clearly, Kant is not going to accept this line of argument, given that he has already rejected the ontological argument. At the same time, he is fully in agreement with the metaphysician that the only way in which theoretical reason could conceive of anything as an absolutely necessary being is if its existence could be thought of as included in its essence. For in no other way could the unconditionally necessary existence of that thing be conceived by our theoretical reason. Since, however, his objections to the ontological argument have shown (as he holds) that it is impossible for existence to be included in the concept of anything whatever, it follows both that the cosmological argument has to rely on the ontological argument to reach its own conclusion and that this conclusion should be rejected.

# The Argument from Design (The Physico-Theological Argument)

*(A 620/B 648–A 630/B 658)*
This argument starts from the actually experienced structure of nature, and attempts to argue from that structure to the existence – even if only highly probable – of God.

Kant is well-disposed towards the Argument from Design, despite holding that it fails to deliver its desired conclusion. He accepts that, given the order, harmony and (apparent) purposiveness in our experience of nature, it is not unreasonable for us to postulate a cause of this nature acting through intelligence and will. From our point of view, it would be unreasonable to hold that, given its harmonious order and complexity, the natural world has arisen from 'blind chance'. (This issue is pursued, in much more detail, in the second half of the *Critique of Judgement*.)

His main objection to the argument is that it simply cannot take us far enough to warrant a justified belief in the *ens realissimum* – which alone, he contends, would be a suitable object of religious belief. For the most that the argument permits us to conclude is a *relatively* powerful, wise and good designer of nature. The argument cannot prove that its designer is *all*-good, *all*-knowing and *all*-powerful (and so, at the same time, capable of being the creator of the materials of nature). Yet, Kant holds, for a reasonable religious belief, we need a proof that such a being must exist. But, if we are to obtain this proof, we will need to leave the Argument from Design and turn, first, to the Cosmological Argument in order to prove the existence of an absolutely necessary being and, then, to the Ontological Argument in order to prove that this necessary being is *all*-powerful, *all*-knowing and *all*-good. In fact, as Kant points out, if the Ontological Argument had been valid, there would have been no need to employ the Argument from Design (or even the Cosmological Argument), since that argument would have proved, in one go, the necessary existence of a being who is *all*-powerful and so on: in sum, a worthy object of religious belief. In so far as a proof of God's existence is sought, by means of pure (theoretical) reason, only the Ontological Argument could have sufficed for this purpose. However, since, on the grounds earlier given, Kant regards this argument as a failure, as well as the Cosmological Argument and the Argument from Design, he concludes that there are no good speculative arguments for God's existence.

Two noteworthy points about Kant's treatment of the Argument from Design are these. First, although he was aware of Hume's criticisms of the argument, he seems not to have taken account of Hume's observation that even if we allow the existence of a designer of the world, we cannot reasonably infer even that this designer is a relatively outstanding one. For we do not know whether this world is the being's first attempt at a design or whether there have been many earlier attempts that have been 'botch'd and bungled' (even admitting that they all obey the universal laws of pure natural science). Second, evolutionary theory – not, of course, seriously considered in Kant's own day – has made less than compelling his claim that the apparent purposiveness that we find in and between natural organisms cannot reasonably be accounted for by us as the natural outcome of the universal empirical laws of physics alone; and that, as a result, we have no option but to ascribe these phenomena to an intelligent cause acting over and beyond any physical laws. (Kant does not maintain that it is impossible for the purposiveness in nature to be explained according to purely physical laws. In fact, he explicitly affirms that we are not entitled to take such a position. But he does hold that we – i.e. human beings – will never be able to account for this purposiveness *without* supposing that it has resulted not from the operation of physical laws alone, but from some further operation of an intelligent cause. In the light of evolutionary theory, even this claim no longer looks attractive.)

Bear in mind that in rejecting all the speculative arguments for God's existence, Kant is not denying that God exists. He is only claiming that there are no valid arguments offered by pure (theoretical) reason to prove *or* disprove God's existence. Metaphysics is simply unable to answer the question of whether God exists, just as it is unable to answer the comparable questions concerning the immortality of the soul and the freedom of the will. Yet Kant does think that we have justified grounds for believing in God – as well as for believing in the immortality of the soul and the freedom of the will. These grounds depend on our *moral* experience rather than upon our *sense* experience.

*

By the end of the *Critique of Pure Reason*, Kant maintains that he has *explained* how there can be synthetic a priori judgements of pure natural science and mathematics as well as provided *proofs* of the fundamental laws lying at the basis of natural science. He also believes he has shown that metaphysics is *unable* to answer any of its own central questions (concerning God, freedom and immortality). The central questions of metaphysics transcend any possible sense experience and, just because this is so, metaphysics itself is powerless to answer them. These – so far – are the main consequences, positive and negative, of Kant's Copernican revolution. It is now time to turn to the fundamentals of his moral philosophy to see whether, with respect to our moral experience, this revolution can lead us to establish what metaphysics itself has been unable to establish.

# PART II

# The Revolution in Ethics – *Groundwork of the Metaphysics of Morals and Critique of Practical Reason*

On the face of it, Kant's account of acting from duty – based on his famous categorical imperative – does not need his Copernican revolution in metaphysics. But this turns out not to be so. As he develops his account, it emerges that his moral system requires that our reason must be free from natural determinism – including all influences from desires and inclinations – and that this is only possible in so far as we make the distinction between the world of appearances and the world of things in themselves (a distinction that is fundamental to his Copernican revolution).

In Chapter 4, Kant's derivation of the categorical imperative will be explained and why he claims that motivation by desires or inclinations can give our actions no true moral worth. Some attempt will also be made to explain why he believes that the categorical imperative, despite being purely formal, can nonetheless tell us determinately what we morally ought to do. The question of how we can ever *act* on the categorical imperative will be taken up in Chapter 5; and an account will be offered of why Kant maintains that while we cannot possibly provide an adequate theoretical answer to this question, his moral system can nonetheless be fully justified from a practical point of view. In Chapter 6, we will see why he believes that the demands of the moral life enable us to prove the existence of God and the immortality of the soul as well as freedom of the will. It is this last idea, *freedom of the will*, which is the pivotal one for the whole of speculative metaphysics – that part of metaphysics which seeks to investigate what transcends our sense experience – and this final chapter ends with a critical discussion of Kant's defence of freedom of the will.

# 4

# The moral law and categorical imperative

The fundamentals of Kant's moral theory – his ethics – are set out in the *Groundwork of the Metaphysics of Morals* (1785) as well as in the Analytic of the *Critique of Practical Reason* (1788). In both, Kant is essentially concerned with identifying what he calls *the supreme principle of morals* and explaining, so far as possible, how this law can apply to us. These are the issues that we shall take up in this chapter and the next one.

For the most part, I will follow the exposition in the *Groundwork* but turn to the *Critique of Practical Reason* when I believe that this can help us with Kant's argument. Almost everyone's first – and frequently only – acquaintance with Kant's ethics comes through the *Groundwork*. That is why, for the purpose of discussing his supreme principle of morals, I am concentrating on that work. Nonetheless, although the *Groundwork* seems to have been envisaged as a simplified account of the basic structure of his moral theory – and generations of students are, for that very reason, introduced to Kant's ethics through the *Groundwork* – it is, in my opinion, a confusing work. I would urge anyone who is finding difficulty in grasping the basic position of the *Groundwork* to read the Analytic of the *Critique of Practical Reason* (especially Chapter I, Sections 1–8: 5:19–33). At the same time, you need to bear in mind that although both essays reach the same or very similar conclusions, the way in which the argument unfolds is rather different in the two cases: that is substantially why I find the exposition in the later work much clearer than in the earlier one.

*

In both the *Groundwork* and *Critique of Practical Reason*, we are introduced to a number of new concepts or, at any rate, to some concepts that have not previously required a technical explanation. Two of them, in particular, are worth identifying straight away. The first is the concept of a *maxim*. A maxim is a practical principle which a rational being is himself acting on or at least seriously proposing to act on (it is not a principle that others are merely suggesting that he follows). It is formulated as a course of action to be *generally* undertaken by the subject under given circumstances (that is why it is a *rule* of action). Examples are: 'When, but only when, it is in my own interest, I shall always serve customers honestly', 'I shall help those in distress whenever I am in a position to do so', 'There are no circumstances in which I shall tell a lie'. A maxim may or may not be a practical principle that is in accordance with morality. (A practical principle itself is any rule of action: it can be a subjective one, that is, a rule that one or more agents are actually acting on – and so a maxim – or it may be an objective one, that is, a law that applies to all possible agents whether or not anyone is actually acting on it.)

The second technical concept is that of the *will*. The will is thought of as a rational being's capacity to be motivated by means of its consciousness of rules of action (made possible by its exercise of reason). For instance, if a rational being has willed a particular action on a given occasion – say the action is that of relieving someone who is starving – this implies that it has both recognized, by employing its reason, that the proposed action falls under an appropriate practical principle, e.g. that everyone should help those in distress whenever the circumstances permit, and been motivated to perform the particular action because reason has recognized the action as an instance of that practical principle.

Kant takes it as a *minimum* condition for a subject to be able to act morally that it can formulate and act on maxims. And since reason is required to formulate any principle or rule of action – and so any maxim – Kant assumes throughout that only rational beings can be moral agents. The question that most concerns him is what *further* conditions need to apply to a rational being if that being is capable of acting morally. We shall find that his concept of *the will* plays a central role in his answer to this question.

## The supreme principle of morals

In the opening section of the *Groundwork*, Kant sets out to discover how we distinguish actions that possess moral worth from those that lack it. He makes what, on the face of it, is the extremely surprising claim that we never think of an action which is solely motivated by a desire or inclination as possessing any genuine moral worth. This is so, he thinks, even if we have employed our reason to determine the best means for attaining the object of our desire *and* the object (or end) thereby achieved is fully in conformity with what is morally good or right. It is only those actions that are performed *irrespective* of whether they achieve, or are even expected to achieve, any desired object (or end) to which we attach moral worth.

Kant is aware that these claims can initially appear strongly counterintuitive. But he is also thinks that, on reflection, we will acknowledge that they are completely in accord with our deepest moral convictions. In order to show this, we are given a number of examples where an agent is himself subject to certain incentives or drives which, as he realizes, may prevent, or at least hinder him from acting virtuously. Clearly such situations are typical of the human predicament. When we are aware of these temptations, we think of the morally right or virtuous action as a *duty*: it is something which, we acknowledge, we morally *ought* to do, whether we in fact do it or not. And what Kant wishes to show is that it is only when the agent's performance of an acknowledged duty is not dependent on *any* desires or inclinations that his action can have moral worth.

Perhaps the most striking, as well as one of the most important, of his examples is the case of an agent who performs an action of helping another in distress out of – entirely out of – a naturally benevolent or sympathetic disposition. Such an action, Kant

maintains, though it is *in conformity with* duty – since it is a duty
(he maintains) to help those in distress when you are in a position
to do so – has no genuine moral worth, however much we may love
the agent for acting on this disposition. And the reason why it has
no moral worth is that the agent has acted from an immediate inclination of sympathy towards another, and not for the sake of duty,
not because the agent has recognized that the action is what, under
the circumstances, he morally ought to do. But, Kant continues,
suppose that this same agent is so borne down by cares of his own
that he entirely loses his natural sympathy for others, and, yet, he
does still help the distressed person – though now *merely* from the
recognition that it is his duty to do so (since, we may suppose, he
is still in a position to provide help). This will be the very first time
that his act of relieving the suffering of others can be conceived as
having any moral worth:

> To help others where one can is a duty, and besides this there are
> many spirits of so sympathetic a temper that, without any further
> motive of vanity or self-interest, they find an inner pleasure in
> spreading happiness around them and can take delight in the
> contentment of others as their own work. Yet I maintain that in
> such a case an action of this kind, however right and however
> amiable it may be, has still no genuinely moral worth ... for its
> maxim lacks moral content, namely, the performance of such
> actions, not from inclination, but *from duty*. Suppose then that
> the mind of this friend of mankind were overclouded by sorrows
> of his own which extinguished all sympathy with the fate of
> others ... and suppose that, when no longer moved by any incli-
> nation, he tears himself out of this deadly insensibility and does
> the action without any inclination for the sake of duty alone;
> then for the first time his action has its genuine moral worth.
>
> (G, Sect. I: 4:398; italics original)

Many readers have been disturbed by this example. It has struck
them as obviously mistaken to affirm that we think of an action
that is wholly motivated by a naturally benevolent disposition as
having *no* genuine moral worth. Simply to claim that this is the case
– as Kant appears to do – looks like begging the question at issue:
the question, namely, of whether we really do think that only to the
extent that an action is performed for the sake of duty, and not on

the basis of any desire or inclination, is it ascribed the *highest*, that is, any *moral*, worth.

In order to appreciate Kant's position here, we need to realize that, as he sees it, if an action arises entirely from a desire or inclination – even one that has as its object the happiness of others – this means that the action has been performed solely for the *pleasure* (or *avoidance of pain*) that it brings to the agent, whether directly or indirectly. In the *Groundwork*, whenever Kant writes of desires or inclinations – elsewhere he sometimes specifies them more narrowly as *sensuous* desires or inclinations – he is always referring to those motives to action which are produced in us by the consciousness of our own pleasure or pain. For example, if I want to visit an Indian restaurant, this desire may have been aroused by the pleasurable prospect (for me) of eating a curry, or if I want to leave a building quickly this may be because I fear its imminent collapse. As Kant sees it, an agent's desire for or aversion to a particular object always results wholly from the pleasure or pain that the agent's consciousness of that object gives to him.

Since, on this picture, the objects of an agent's desires or inclinations are determined by their tendency (actual or believed) to increase his own pleasure or avoidance of pain, Kant affirms that whenever we act on our desires or inclinations, we are each, to that extent, only governed by considerations of self-love or our own happiness: by what, in the *Critique of Practical Reason*, he calls 'the general principle of self-love' (*CPractR*, Bk I, Chap. I, Sects 2 and 3; 5:21–2). And, he further maintains, no action which is performed purely from the motive of self-love can have any moral worth, however useful the action may be to the wider community.

I think that most of us would agree that in so far as an action is motivated purely by self-love, or the thought of one's own happiness, it can have no moral worth. What is plainly more contentious is whether Kant is correct in maintaining that all actions that are motivated by desires or inclinations – *including* those that are motivated by sympathy or benevolence towards others – are, to that extent, the product of self-love. Kant undoubtedly believes that they are. For, as I have already noted, he thinks that these actions are solely determined by the pleasure to the agent that their performance, or the thought of their performance, produces. So, in the particular example of the agent with the sympathetic temperament, although we are told that he has no *further* motive of 'vanity or self-interest', we are also told that he finds an 'inner pleasure' and 'delight' in spreading happiness to others; and the implication is that it is this pleasure which is actually motivating the agent. In fact, in the *Critique of Practical Reason*, Kant explicitly maintains that whenever any of us is motivated to perform a given action by a desire or inclination, this always results from the pleasure (or avoidance of pain) that the thought of the action gives to the agent and, hence, from the motive of self-love (*CPractR*, Chap. I, Sects 2–3: 5:21–2).

Note that although, in the first part of the story of the sympathetic agent, there is no further or ulterior end that he desires in spreading happiness to others, there is a desired end or object. This end is the happiness of others; and, according to Kant, the desire for it is generated precisely because the thought of spreading happiness to those currently in distress gives the agent pleasure. Hence, this is an example where an agent's performance of an action *directly* contributes (as he believes) to satisfying his desire. Of course, many actions are performed only, or mainly, because they *indirectly* contribute to the satisfaction of a desire. For instance, if an agent has the desired end of being a successful politician, he may spend time studying economics. His reason, we may suppose, shows him that acquiring knowledge of economics is an important *means* to satisfying his long-term desire to be a successful politician. Here, the study of economics is believed by him indirectly to contribute to the satisfaction of that desire. Moreover, if we suppose that the thought of studying economics gives him no immediate pleasure, he will undertake the study merely so that (as he believes) it will increase his chances of being a successful politician. It is this hoped for achievement that the agent ultimately desires because it is the thought of being a successful politician which gives him pleasure – and it is the consciousness of this pleasure which indirectly motivates him to study economics.

Let me summarize the main grounds that Kant has so far offered for distinguishing acting for the sake of duty from acting on desires or inclinations. Actions that are wholly prompted by desires or inclinations – even when the actions are fully in accord with duty (as in the example of the sympathetic agent) – can possess no moral worth. For such actions are only performed for the pleasure or avoidance of pain that they are believed to bring, either directly or indirectly, to the agent. Yet, in our moral consciousness, we make a clear and decisive distinction between acting from duty and acting from self-love (for our own pleasure or avoidance of pain). Accordingly, in so far as an action is performed for the sake of duty, it cannot depend on anything that relies for its motivational effect on stimulating the agent's desires or inclinations. On the contrary, to the extent that the action can have any moral worth, the motivation of the action must be independent of everything that can contribute to their stimulation. For if, to the extent to which an action possesses moral worth, its motivation must not rely on any stimulation from desires or inclinations, the basis of the agent's moral motivation must be independent of everything that can serve to generate his desires or inclinations.

The upshot is that what the agent needs to do, in order to determine if his contemplated action can have any moral worth, is to see whether its maxim is one that he can will even when it makes *no* appeal to his desires or inclinations. This he can discover if he asks himself whether he can will the maxim as a law holding for all *possible* rational beings, i.e. *whatever* differences there could be in their desires and inclinations (throughout Kant is referring only to finite rational beings who possess a will). For the only thing that all possible rational beings have in common is their capacity to exercise reason. So if an agent acts on his maxim only in so far as he can will it as a law holding for all possible rational beings, the maxim cannot, to that extent, be making any appeal to his desires or inclinations. It cannot, because there is no object that can stimulate the desires or inclinations of all possible rational beings; and, hence, the content of his maxim – its specification of a particular action – cannot stimulate the desires or inclinations of all of them. It is at best an empirical generalization that all actual rational beings desire the same object (including the same particular action): such a generalization could not hold for all possible rational beings. Consequently, if an agent acts on his maxim only in so far as he can will that all other possible rational beings also do, his motivation cannot result from anything about the maxim which is capable of stimulating his desires or inclinations. For if there were, it would equally have to stimulate the desires or inclinations of every other possible rational being – and this is impossible, given that there is no object that can stimulate the desires of all of them.

Accordingly, if the agent acts only in so far as his maxim can be willed by all possible rational beings, his action cannot be motivated by anything about his maxim that appeals to his desires or inclinations. His motivation must, rather, come from the mere recognition that the maxim is one that can be adopted as a law by all possible rational beings. In other words, once we have entirely laid aside a maxim's content, in the manner just described, nothing remains to motivate the will *except* the possibility that it can be willed by all possible rational beings. Hence, to the extent to which an action is performed for the sake of duty, it must be the mere *form* of the agent's practical principle – more especially, that his maxim can be willed as a universal law (i.e. as one holding for all possible rational beings) – and not its *content* that motivates his will.

This is not to deny that an agent may *also* will the action because the content of his maxim pleases him. But in so far as his action has any moral worth, it must be motivated by the thought that he can will the maxim as a universal law. This motivation alone entails that the agent's performance of the action is not dependent on any of his desires or inclinations and it alone confers moral worth on his action. For once we have eliminated all motivation by desires or inclinations, nothing is left to motivate the will and to provide an action with moral worth – which we undoubtedly acknowledge that some actions can possess – except the maxim's mere conformity to universal law. This conformity, since it concerns the mere structure or form of the agent's maxim, can be determined only by reason.

Kant has now arrived at *the supreme principle of morals* – what he more often calls *the moral law* or *categorical imperative* – under which the maxim of any action must fall if the action itself is to be performed for the sake of duty. In so far as an action can have any moral worth, it must be performed because the agent's maxim – his own principle of action – can, at the same time, be willed as a universal law:

> But what kind of law can this be the thought of which, even without regard to the results expected from it, has to determine the will if this is to be called good absolutely and without quali-fication? Since I have robbed the will of every inducement that might arise for it as a consequence of obeying any particular law, nothing is left but the conformity of actions to universal law as such, and this alone must serve the will as its principle. That is to say, I ought never to act except in such a way *that I can also will that my maxim should become a universal law*. Here bare

conformity to universal law as such (without having as its base any law prescribing particular actions) is what serves the will as its principle, and must so serve it if duty is not to be everywhere an empty delusion and chimerical concept.

*(G, Sect. I: 4:402; italics original)*

# Form and content: reason and sentiment

In outlining his derivation of the moral law or categorical imperative, I have employed Kant's own distinction between the *content* and *form* of a practical principle. It is now time to say something further about this distinction and to place it in a wider philosophical context.

The content of a principle refers to what it is about – its *subject matter* – whether this is (for instance) alleviating the suffering of others or improving one's own worldly standing. When an agent acts on a principle because its content is motivating his will, Kant calls the practical principle a *material* one. And, as we have seen, he thinks that *all* material principles motivate the will solely by means of the pleasure or pain that the principles' content brings to the agent himself: it is these sensations of pleasure or pain that give rise to our desires and inclinations. On the other hand, when an agent acts on a principle in virtue of its mere form or structure, he calls the practical principle a purely *formal* one. Only a formal principle can motivate the will independently of any feelings of pleasure or pain. For a principle that motivates the will in virtue of its form, and not its content, arouses no feelings that stimulate a desire or aversion for an object. Such feelings are only aroused by what can be given in the content of a principle, not by what is wholly dependent on our reason in order to be known, as with the mere form or structure of a principle. On this issue, there is unanimity between those philosophers, like Kant, who claim that morality is founded on reason alone (they are known as ethical rationalists) and those philosophers, like Hume, who claim that morality must be founded on sentiment or feeling as well as reason (they are known as ethical empiricists). Both parties agree that the exercise of reason – here taken to include the understanding – does not produce *by itself* any feelings that can motivate the will. This position is well summed up by Hume in his *An Enquiry concerning the Principles of Morals*:

> The end of all moral speculations is to teach us our duty and, by proper representations of the deformity of vice and beauty of virtue, beget correspondent habits, and engage us to avoid the one, and embrace the other. But is this ever to be expected from inferences or conclusions of the understanding [or reason], which of themselves have no hold on the affections ... ?
>
> *(Sect. I)*

Since Hume contended that the exercise of reason does not, by itself, give rise to any feelings of pleasure or pain – and certainly none that stimulates a desire or aversion for an object – he concluded that reason alone cannot be the foundation of morality, granting (as Kant also would have done) that morality is a 'practical study', i.e. is essentially concerned with *acting* for the sake of duty. Morality for Hume must be founded on the stimulation of our feelings as well as on the use of our reason.

Kant is radically opposed to this conception of the foundations of morality. He has maintained that if an action is performed for the sake of duty, it cannot, to that extent, be motivated by the pleasure, or avoidance of pain, that its performance, or the thought of its performance, brings to the agent. An action can have moral worth only in so far as the principle on which we act motivates us not in virtue of its *content* (or *matter*) but in virtue of its *form* (or *structure*) alone – more particularly, in virtue of its capacity to be willed as a universal law. Now the question of whether a practical principle can be willed as a universal law is determined by *reason* (since it is reason that determines the form or structure of a principle). It must, therefore, be our reason that determines our duties *and* fundamentally motivates the will, if our actions are to have any moral worth.

There is a salient point about Kant's strategy in the *Groundwork* that it is all too easy to miss. Nothing he argues for in Section I or Section II of that work is intended to prove that reason alone *can* motivate the will. For all that is said up until at least the end of Section II, Hume may be correct in affirming that reason alone is unable to motivate the will. What Kant has maintained is that IF duty is not 'everywhere to be an empty delusion and a chimerical concept', it must be possible for us to act only on those maxims that we can will as universal laws (and, hence, can will through reason alone). Thus, as Kant sees it, any 'moral' theory – like Hume's – which claims that we cannot motivate our actions by means of reason alone, and that the performance of our duties is ultimately founded on feeling (or sentiment), utterly annihilates the very possibility of our actions having any genuine moral worth. In the *Groundwork*, it will not be until the final section, Section III, that Kant takes up the key question of how, if at all, pure reason – reason alone – can be practical, i.e. motivate the will.

# The feeling of respect

Although Kant claims unambiguously that acting for the sake of duty requires that one must be fundamentally motivated by reason to the exclusion of any desires or inclinations, he also – and seemingly inconsistently – claims that to act from duty requires that one is conscious of acting out of *respect* (or *reverence*) for the moral law. And, in maintaining this, he asserts that respect is a *feeling*. So it appears that he is saying both that we must act on reason alone and that we must act on a feeling (of respect) if we are to act for the sake of duty. This looks wildly paradoxical, the more so given all that he has previously affirmed – and will subsequently affirm – about the need to set aside any feelings of pleasure or pain, any feelings of compassion or tender sympathy, that may intrude upon the exercise of reason in motivating us to do our duty.

What is said in the *Groundwork* concerning the relation between acting on reason alone and acting out of respect for the moral law has understandably puzzled many of its readers. If we are to resolve the puzzlement, we need to keep the following point firmly in mind: Kant is definitely not retracting his claim that reason must fundamentally motivate the will, if there are to be any acts of moral worth. No feeling, or set of feelings, can *precede* the exercise of reason and be the ground – the only ground – of motivation, if an agent is to act for the sake of duty. How then can the feeling of respect play a part in our moral motivation?

Kant's answer is a good deal clearer in the *Critique of Practical Reason* (see *CPractR*, Bk I, Chap. III, 'Of the incentives of pure practical reason': 5:71–89). But even in the *Groundwork*, it does emerge that the feeling of respect *results from* the exercise of pure reason in formulating and seeking to act on a universal law: it is not that we first experience the feeling of respect which then causes our reason to formulate and perhaps act on a law. Far from it: 'reverence [or respect] is regarded as the *effect* of the law on the subject and not as the *cause* of the law' (*G*, Sect. I; 4:401, footnote; italics original). The feeling of respect is the consciousness, at the phenomenal level, of our exercising pure practical reason *against* our desires and inclinations. Pure reason, therefore, is the fundamental motivating force whenever we act for the sake of duty; but we become conscious of its action on the will by means of the feeling of respect that reason produces as it *opposes* our desires and inclinations. So the exercise of reason by itself does not give rise to any feeling – it does not by itself, as Hume put it, 'have any hold on our affections' – but it does, nonetheless, give rise to our feeling of respect for the moral law by means of its constraining tendency on our desires and inclinations.

As finite rational beings, our will is always susceptible to determination by desires and inclinations – in fact, in any given practical situation, Kant maintains that the influence of these impulses always makes itself known to us *first* – and this influence on our will is opposed by reason alone (on the basis of its application of the moral law to the given situation). The opposition of these two different determining grounds, together with our recognition that it is reason's inference from the moral law that ought to prevail, is made known to us by the feeling of respect for the moral law. This feeling is the product of pure practical reason's resistance to the will being motivated by our desires or inclinations (the empirical determining grounds of the will); and testifies to our rational nature's acknowledgement of the authority of the moral law. The following passage from the *Critique of Practical Reason* highlights these points:

> The dissimilarity of determining grounds (empirical and rational) is made known by this resistance of a practical lawgiving reason to every meddling inclination, by a special kind of *feeling*, which, however, does not precede the lawgiving of practical reason but is instead only produced by it and indeed as a constraint, namely through the feeling of respect such as no human being has for inclination of whatever kind but does for the [moral] law.
>
> (*CPractR, 5:92; italics original*)

Accordingly, when we *do* act out of respect for the moral law, it is our pure practical reason that has provided the will's motivation, and the action will, as a result, have been performed for the sake of duty. However, since we frequently fail so to act on occasions when we should, Kant expresses the relationship between the feeling of respect and our duty by saying that '*Duty is the necessity to act out of respect for the law*' (G, Sect. I: 4:400; italics original). In witnessing or imagining a morally fine action, we recognize the overriding requirement – the necessity – to act out of the respect we then feel for the moral law. Yet this feeling is itself the *consequence* of the exercise of reason alone opposing our empirically determined will; and, to the extent that our actions have any moral worth, it must be the exercise of pure reason that succeeds in motivating the will (by overcoming our desires and inclinations).

# How can the categorical imperative tell us what we ought to do?

So far, we have looked at how Kant arrives at the moral law or categorical imperative as the supreme principle of morals and how he thinks we become conscious of that law's authority over us, viz. through the feeling of respect. We have also broached, but not resolved, the question of how morality can exist at all if reason alone must be capable of motivating the will. This, as we noted, is a question that Hume had raised against any version of ethical rationalism. And he rejected that theory wholesale on the grounds that reason alone is incapable of moving us to action: any viable moral theory must make reference to our sentiments and, thereby, to our desires and inclinations in order to account for the *practical* nature of morality. I think it is fair to say that this objection is the most significant one confronting Kant's ethics. We will return to it.

In fact, Hume had what he regarded as *two* decisive objections to ethical rationalism. These are: 1) Reason alone is incapable of *determining* our duties; 2) Reason alone is incapable of *motivating the will* (to do our duties). It is the second of these objections that I have just been alluding to. But what of the first objection: that reason alone cannot even tell us what our duties are – quite apart from whether it can motivate us to act on them?

It has been a perennial criticism of the categorical imperative that its purely *formal* nature effectively disables it from delivering any sufficiently determinate judgements about what we morally ought to do. I cannot discuss this issue in any depth in this brief study. At the same time, we must make an attempt to understand why Kant plainly did believe that the categorical imperative could tell us, quite specifically, what our duties are. A preliminary point is, however, worth making before we look at some of his examples. In maintaining that we use the categorical imperative in day-to-day situations, he is not supposing that we *explicitly* employ this rule every time we ask ourselves what we morally ought to do (any more than he thinks that we must have explicitly employed the principle of sufficient reason every time we take ourselves to perceive an objective change of state). Nonetheless, he does believe that our *practice* in moral situations shows evidently that, at an implicit level, we always do employ the categorical imperative in order to find out our duty.

It is in Section II of the *Groundwork* that Kant endeavours to explain most clearly and succinctly the general framework governing how the categorical imperative operates in actual cases. He does so by taking four examples where an agent asks himself whether, if he acts on a given maxim, his action could have moral worth. I shall consider two of the four examples: these differ in an instructive respect. The other two examples, although they do illustrate additional differences between maxims, do not add anything to the important difference that I want primarily to bring out. (I shall, however, consider one of the further examples – concerning suicide – in the ensuing discussion.)

The first case – also discussed in Section I – is that of a subject who is resolved to act on the maxim that in order to borrow money when in financial difficulty, he will make a promise to repay the debt *even though* he intends never to fulfil his promise. We can take it that the agent has calculated that such behaviour would be in his overall self-interest: the question that remains is whether it is morally right. In order to find the answer, the agent needs to ask himself if he can will the maxim as a universal law: that is, as a rule which it is accepted that every rational being is permitted to act on. Once the maxim is transformed into a universal law, it transpires that there is no possibility that a lying promise, concerning the repayment of money, can succeed, provided it is known that the agent is in financial difficulty. If the maxim is to operate as a universal law, it is necessary that those to whom the promise is made believe the profession to repay the debt. But, granting they realize that the agent is in financial difficulty, they will not believe it. The maxim cannot therefore stand as a universal law.

Bear in mind that we are assuming that the following principle holds or is accepted as a universal law: it is permissible to make a lying promise when in financial difficulty. Since, *ex hypothesi*, it is in the agent's perceived self-interest to make a lying promise, and since (as Kant holds) everybody always acts, and is taken to act, in their own perceived self-interest *unless* deflected from doing so by the recognition that the action is morally prohibited, it follows that we can be certain that the agent is lying, provided we know that he is in financial difficulty. We can be certain that he is lying because it is accepted that such action is not morally prohibited. Accordingly, the maxim cannot be conceived to operate as a universal law, since a condition for its operating, viz. that others believe the agent's profession to repay though he is in financial difficulty, will not obtain. As Kant puts it, if the maxim became a universal law, 'it would make promising, and the very purpose of promising, itself impossible [in cases of financial difficulty], since no one would believe he was being promised anything, but would laugh at utterances of this kind as empty shams'(G, 4:422).

A second type of case is illustrated by a comfortably situated agent who adopts the maxim never to help those whom he can relieve from distress, on the grounds that the good or ill fortune of others is no concern to him. This maxim, Kant acknowledges, unlike the maxim in the first type of case can be *conceived* as a universal law but it cannot be *willed* as such. A society that is governed by mutual self-interest – and in which no one comes to the aid of those who are unable, by ill fortune, to engage in acts of mutual self-interest – can be conceived as continuing in existence. But this state of affairs cannot be willed by the agent as a universal law. It cannot because, in order to test whether his maxim is opposed to duty, the agent has to consider those situations where he finds himself in distress and where there are others who could help him. For if a situation is morally right, it is so when the roles of the beings in the given situation are reversed, assuming there is no relevant difference between them. When the comfortably situated agent attempts to reverse the roles, i.e. by imagining himself in a situation of distress and others, who are comfortably situated, in a position to help him, it turns out that he cannot will his maxim as a universal law. As a finite rational being, he necessarily has needs (this is part of the meaning of a *finite* rational being: unlike God who has no needs): more especially, the need to avoid unnecessary pain and to obtain happiness. Accordingly, in a condition of distress, he requires – and, so through his reason, he wills – the aid of others. Yet, since he can conceive his original maxim as a universal law, he *also* wills that every rational being accepts the rule that no one is to help those in distress, even when in a position to do so. Hence, his will is in contradiction with itself: the agent has willed both that no one comes to his aid and that someone does. Note that this case is not an appeal to self-interest but merely to the demands of reason. The comfortably situated agent may fully appreciate – and certainly have no doubt – that there is no realistic prospect of his ever finding himself in serious distress and needing the help of others. It is, nonetheless, a logical demand of morality that he test his maxim to see if it can be willed as a universal law; and his reason shows him that it cannot be.

So we have two types of maxim, those that cannot even be conceived as universal laws and those that cannot be willed as such. (Evidently, if a maxim cannot be conceived as a universal law, it cannot be willed as a universal law either. So when Kant affirms that the categorical imperative entails that you act only on those maxims that you can, at the same time, will as universal laws, this should be taken to rule out acting on those maxims that cannot even be conceived as universal laws.) Whatever else may be said about Kant's categorical imperative, it is, I hope, clear from these examples that its formal nature is compatible with delivering rules forbidding *specific* types of action. What is sometimes overlooked is that each of us, as finite rational beings, already has many specific desires and needs. These are felt *before* we employ the categorical imperative to decide on our duties: and, for each of us, our original maxims are the formulation of those rules of action which are expressive of our personal desires as well as our needs. There are, therefore, *many* specific types of maxim that each of us are going to act on unless the recognition of our duty restrains us – and it is on these specific maxims that the categorical imperative is exercised in order to determine our duties. Each of the above examples shows that attempting to universalize one's maxims can indeed deliver specific moral prohibitions. Admittedly, very many maxims can be *conceived* as universal laws; but the additional constraint that one must be able to *will* a maxim as a universal law has considerable restrictive force. Asking oneself whether, if the roles are reversed in a situation, one can still consistently will the universalizing of one's maxim clearly does further limit which maxims one can adopt as universal laws.

However, it may now be objected that what we have found is that the categorical imperative can deliver, but *only* deliver, moral prohibitions. It gives us no guidance as to what we *positively* ought to do in any situation: it only manages to *rule out* certain types of action. Although, in the *Groundwork*, Kant is not as forthright as he might be in explicitly countering this objection, it is clear enough from what he says elsewhere that the objection is misguided. Consider both the first type of example where a maxim cannot even be conceived as a universal law and the second where it cannot be willed as such. Since, in both, the actions enjoined in the maxims are morally *prohibited* (because the maxims cannot stand as universal laws), Kant holds that the opposite action is a *duty*. So, in our first example, since it is impossible to conceive the maxim of making a lying promise, under the given circumstances, holding as a universal law, the action enjoined in the maxim is prohibited in every case *and* it is a duty only to make a promise, under those circumstances, where there is the intention to repay the debt. In the second example, since it is impossible to will as a universal law the maxim of not helping others in distress when in a position to do so, the action enjoined is morally prohibited *and* it is a duty to help others in distress provided one is in a position to.

If there is no contradiction in universalizing a maxim or its opposite, both the corresponding actions are morally *permitted*. It is sometimes said that because the categorical imperative does not always discriminate between two opposing ways of behaving, it fails in its task. But this objection appears to assume that of two diametrically opposed courses of action, one of them must always be the morally right one. That is not obviously correct; and unless it is shown to be so, it cannot be an objection to Kant's categorical imperative that it makes room for two opposing courses of action as morally permitted. Moreover, it follows from accepting moral permissions, that a given course of action cannot be correctly

pronounced morally wrong, if the categorical imperative shows
that the maxim enjoining the action and its opposite can both
be universalized. So, even here, the categorical imperative is able
to show that a course of action is not morally wrong – and may,
therefore, be performed without contravening duty.

There is one further criticism that I will take up. This is the
familiar one that Kant's conception of a duty is unrealistically
*universal*: if some action is right, it is *always* right, and if it is
wrong, it is *always* wrong. Kant's position on truth-telling is
usually taken to show his acceptance of this thesis. Admittedly, he
does seem to hold that one ought always to tell the truth: there
are no circumstances where a 'white lie' is in order. At the same
time, it is not evident that his moral theory commits him to this
unrestricted position even with regard to truth-telling, as various
commentators have observed. But, in any case, it is patently
mistaken to suppose that he thinks that our duties are invariably
similarly unrestricted. Consider another of his four examples in
Section II of the *Groundwork*: the example of the agent who is
contemplating suicide. As with the previously discussed case of
making a lying promise in order to extricate oneself from financial
difficulty, Kant argues that it is impossible even to conceive the
maxim of committing suicide out of self-love as a universal law.
Accordingly, he maintains that suicide out of self-love is *always*
prohibited. But he does not maintain that *suicide* – or, what he
terms, the deliberate killing of oneself – is always prohibited. A
maxim not only contains a description of the proposed act broadly
conceived, e.g. committing suicide or making a lying promise, but
that of its grounds or motive, e.g. out of self-love or in order to
extricate oneself from financial difficulty. So, when specified more
particularly, the actions prescribed in maxims contain a reference
to the grounds or motive. It is these more specific descriptions that
the agent is required to universalize in order to determine the moral
status of his proposed actions.

Whereas Kant holds that suicide *out of self-love* is morally
prohibited, he grants that suicide *in order to prevent a secret falling
into the hands of your country's enemies* is morally permissible (see
*The Metaphysics of Morals*, Part II: The Metaphysical Principles
of Virtue, First Part, Sections 5 and 6: 6:421–3). He thinks that
a maxim licensing suicide out of self-love cannot be conceived as
holding universally in a system of nature. It cannot because (Kant

claims) the function of self-love is to preserve one's life wherever possible; and this is directly opposed to a system of nature where self-love functions to end one's life when its continuation 'seems to threaten more evil than it promises satisfaction'. (His idea appears to be that if, under the given circumstances, suicide out of self-love held as a *universal* law, it would give to the inclination of self-love two functions which are directly opposed: one in which the inclination always naturally strives to preserve one's life and another in which, under some of the same circumstances, it naturally strives to end it. It is impossible to conceive a system of nature, i.e. a system governed by universal laws, operating in this way.) But the maxim to commit suicide in order not to give away secrets to your country's enemies, e.g. as a result of torture, can be willed as a universal law. It is, therefore, not contrary to duty.

Whatever one thinks of the merits of Kant's particular argument in the case of suicide, it is clear that his employment of the categorical imperative does not have the implausible implication that actions that are morally right or wrong, under certain circumstances, are necessarily so in all circumstances. The grounds or motive have to be taken into account in asking whether one's maxim can hold as a universal law, and this may considerably restrict the scope of the universal law (just as it is a universal law that water boils at 100 degrees C, *provided* the pressure is normal).

I conclude that Hume's *first* objection to ethical rationalism – namely, that reason alone cannot *determine* what is morally right or wrong – is not obviously decisive against Kant's moral theory. Since, on the latter's theory, reason's employment of the categorical imperative is addressed to an agent's proposed, and usually quite specific, practical rule (a maxim), it would, in principle, seem possible for reason to determine whether the consequent action can or cannot be performed for the sake of duty. Furthermore, the examples which Kant gives, in the *Groundwork*, to illustrate how the categorical imperative operates, strongly suggest that, at least in *some* cases, reason actually is able to tell us what is morally right or wrong.

This leaves us with the *second* of Hume's major objections to any rationalist theory of ethics, viz. that even if reason can determine what actions are virtuous and what are vicious, it cannot alone *motivate* the will to produce virtuous acts and avoid vicious ones. It is only if our desires or inclinations are stimulated – by the prospect of pleasure or pain – that our will can be engaged to act on any rules: rules that stipulate what we *ought* to do. But *these* rules always tell us what we ought to do in order to obtain what we desire or avoid what we fear; they tell us the best *means* to attain the presumed objects of pleasure or avoid the presumed objects of pain. 'Extinguish all the warm feelings and prepossessions in favour of virtue, and all disgust and aversion to vice ... and morality is no longer a practical study, nor has any tendency to regulate our lives and actions' (*An Enquiry concerning the Principles of Morals*, Sect. I). Even *if* reason could determine what is virtuous and vicious, unless our feelings are touched and, thereby, provide the initial impetus to action, morality – as a practical discipline – will be at an end. This Humean position is manifestly a major challenge to Kant since, according to him, unless reason alone *can* be practical, there can be no such thing as morality at all.

# 5

# Can reason motivate the will?

Near the end of Section II of the *Groundwork*, Kant summarizes the most notable differences between his version of ethical rationalism and, in effect, Hume's version of ethical empiricism. (He compares his own position with a number of other moral theories too, but it is his comparison with Hume's theory that I want to focus on.) He compares the two theories by employing his distinction, introduced here for the first time, between autonomy and heteronomy of the will. This distinction is itself closely connected to another that is also introduced in Section II, namely, the distinction between categorical and hypothetical imperatives. Understanding these two distinctions should help us come to grips with the main issue of this chapter: What is Kant's answer to the question of how reason alone can be practical?

## The distinction between autonomy and heteronomy of the will and its relationship with categorical and hypothetical imperatives

Where there is *autonomy* of the will, reason employs the categorical imperative to determine what we ought to do and motivates the will accordingly. The will is here motivated by the *self-legislation* of reason, i.e. by reason employing a rule entirely of its own devising (the categorical imperative), and hence reason is operating quite independently of any desires or inclinations. This contrasts with *heteronomy* of the will where the motivation comes not from the exercise of reason, but from the agent's desires or inclinations. Here, reason merely determines the best *means* for attaining any desired object (or end) – and a desire or inclination always precedes reason's formulation of a rule of action and provides the motivation of the will.

Only in so far as the will is working autonomously can the agent's actions have any moral worth; for it is only then that the mere conformity of his maxims to the categorical imperative motivates his will. Heteronomy of the will is opposed to morally commendable acts because even when the actions produced are in accordance with duty, the will's motivation comes not from the recognition that one's maxims can be willed as universal laws – and so not from reason alone – but from desires or inclinations. Although the agent may here be acting *in conformity with* duty, he is not acting *for the sake of* duty: this requires that the actions arise from autonomy of the will.

The distinction between autonomy and heteronomy of the will can now be used to contrast the fundamentals of Kant's ethical rationalism with Hume's ethical empiricism. On the Kantian view, all moral ought judgements arise immediately from the agent's use of reason (in determining whether the proposed maxims can be willed as universal laws). They state what the agent ought to do *whatever* his desires or inclinations may urge: that is why Kant calls them *categorical* imperatives. And in so far as our actions have any moral worth, they must be motivated by reason's immediate recognition that they ought to be done. In that way alone can the actions be performed for the sake of duty. If it is claimed that an action ought to be done *because* it is the best means for accomplishing some desired end (even if that end is e.g. the avoidance of suffering in others), it can have, to that extent, no moral worth: its performance may manifest a will that is in conformity with duty, but not a will that has acted for the sake of duty. Consequently, for Kant, all actions that are performed for the sake of duty manifest and must manifest *autonomy* of the will.

On the Humean view, all ought judgements – *including* moral ones

– only arise mediately (not immediately) from the use of reason. They state what the agent ought to do *if* he has certain desires or inclinations: that is why Kant calls them *hypothetical* imperatives. Reason is here employed only to discover the best means for obtaining the objects (or ends) desired. Hence, our recognition that an action ought morally to be done is always conditional upon certain of the agent's desires or inclinations; and the role of reason is only to work out what we ought to do *in order to* attain the objects of our desires. But it is our desires for these ends that precede the operation of reason in determining what we ought to do, and it is one or more of these desires, not our reason, that invariably motivates the will. According to Hume, therefore, all actions that are performed from duty manifest and can only manifest *heteronomy* of the will.

Kant believes that as an *analysis* of what we everyday understand by acting from duty, the Humean position is quite simply mistaken. He believes that his analysis of such everyday concepts as *duty* and *moral obligation* has shown plainly that we *contrast* acting from duty with acting for some desired end (whatever it may be), and that if morality is to be a practical discipline, reason alone must both determine our duties and motivate the will to perform them. If morality is not to be 'an empty delusion', we need to act from autonomy and not heteronomy of the will.

That is all very well, you may say, but HOW is it even *possible* for an agent to motivate his will by reason alone? And, equally to the point, HOW – on Kant's conception of *duty* – can we acknowledge the *necessity* of acting for the sake of duty, even when we can see, perfectly well, that such an action may not only fail to serve our self-interest but actually militate against it? For, as Kant has argued, our ordinary notions of *duty* and *moral obligation* undoubtedly carry with them this uncompromising directive. Yet, throughout his intricate analysis of these notions (as set out in Sections I and II of the *Groundwork*), we have been given no explanation of how it is even possible for pure reason to be practical, let alone how the moral law can be recognized as having *supreme authority* over all our actions, i.e. as telling us what we *ought* to do, irrespective of our desires and inclinations.

It is, at this juncture that Kant turns to his Copernican revolution in metaphysics, with its distinction between the world of appearances (the phenomenal world) and the world of things in themselves (the noumenal world).

# How is the categorical imperative possible?

We have seen that, for Kant, autonomy of the will is necessary if morality is to be a going concern. But how is autonomy of the will possible – that is, how can reason alone motivate the will?

Kant argues that our concept of *freedom* is the key to understanding how this is possible. After all, a will that is free is one that operates independently of any determination from alien (or outside) causes and which, at the same time, is itself the cause of actions. But if we are to conceive of anything as capable of causality, we need to think of it as acting in accordance with a law: a law that includes within it the idea that if something, the cause, exists, something else *always* exists as a consequence (under the same circumstances). The very concept of *cause* carries with it the idea of this lawful connection. So a free will cannot operate lawlessly, if it is to be capable of exercising causality with respect to actions. It must, rather, be governed wholly by means of a law of its own: it must be *self*-determined (give rise to actions *of itself*) and not be determined to produce actions by alien (or outside) causes.

Now since the will is the capacity of a rational being to be motivated through its consciousness of rules of action (and so by its exercise of reason), a free will must be a will that is motivated by reason alone: only then is the will motivated through its own capacity. If the rule of action is dependent for its motivational power on alien causes (desires or inclinations), the will cannot be motivating *itself* to produce the action (i.e. by means of reason) and so cannot be willing freely. Consequently, the rule governing a free will must be formulated by reason in such a way that it precisely *excludes* any determination of the will by alien causes, that is, by any desires or inclinations. For these impulses arise *independently* of reason and, hence, in so far as the will is determined by them, it is being determined by alien causes and not by a rule of its own making. But, as we have already discovered, the only practical rule that lays aside any determination of the will by desires and inclinations is the one that enjoins the agent always to act only on a maxim that can at the same time be willed as a universal law: in other words, the moral law or categorical imperative. All other practical rules are *material* ones (they motivate in virtue of their *content*), and, as such, they can only motivate the will by means of desires or inclinations. In short, the will can be conceived as both free from determination by desires and inclinations (alien causes) and, at the same time, itself the cause of actions – and, hence, be a *free will* – only in so far as it is governed by a rule formulated by reason alone. This rule of action is the moral law. That is why Kant concludes: 'Thus a free will and a will under moral laws are one and the same'.

We can now *in a sense* understand how autonomy of the will is possible: it is possible if the will can be free. If a rational being is to act for the sake of duty, it must be capable of willing autonomously; and this, in turn, requires that it can will freely.

But are we capable of willing freely? Kant's answer, originally given in the *Critique of Pure Reason* and merely sketched out in Section III of the *Groundwork*, is that it is at least not logically impossible for us to possess this capacity, but *only* in so far as we distinguish the world of appearances (the spatio-temporal or phenomenal world) from the world as it is in itself (the non-spatial and non-temporal or noumenal world). For without this distinction, everything that happens in the spatio-temporal world must be thought of as determined, and only determined, by earlier events in the temporal series; and, in the case of an agent, every action must be conceived as caused by desires or inclinations (which themselves arise from the thought of pleasure or pain). All our actions would be the result of *heteronomy* of the will, just as Hume held, and none could manifest autonomy of the will. However, if the agent can be conceived, at least in respect of his possession of reason and a will, as having an existence in the noumenal world, then there would be no contradiction in supposing that his will can be motivated by reason alone and, hence, *independently* of any desires or inclinations. Freedom and autonomy of the will would be logically possible, and an agent's actions could have genuine moral worth.

In this way, Kant replies to the first of our two questions, that of 'How is it even possible for reason alone to motivate the will?' By distinguishing between the phenomenal and noumenal worlds, and by locating reason and the will in the noumenal world, we can admit that our will is free *in so far as* it is motivated by the categorical imperative (reason alone). And Kant further argues that each of us does, in fact, acknowledge that we really are capable of performing free acts. For we think of ourselves as possessing a will; that is, a faculty which is itself capable of producing actions on the basis of the consciousness of rules (and, hence, through the exercise of reason). But it is impossible to conceive of the will as possessing this causality with respect to actions *unless* we presuppose freedom of the will. For if the will could never be motivated by reason alone, and was, instead, inevitably determined to act by alien causes – and, more particularly, by desires and inclinations – we could not regard our will as itself capable of exercising *any* causality. We could not because the most that reason would here be doing is simply acting as the servant or slave of these impulsions, i.e. in working out the best *means* for obtaining our desired ends. The causality of the actions themselves would *not* come from the will but from desires or inclinations. Yet, it is quite evident that we do regard ourselves as possessing a will, as can be seen from our readiness to praise or blame ourselves and others for acting or failing to act for the sake of duty (and so on the basis of reason alone). However, this very commitment to our possession of a will – to our possession of a faculty which is itself capable of exercising causality with respect to actions – shows that we must equally be committed to possessing freedom of the will.

Kant expresses this last observation by saying that 'from a practical point of view' we really are free (*G*, Sect. III; 4:448). What he means by this is not that he has proved, on theoretical grounds, that we are capable of willing freely (for instance, by simply *analysing* our concepts of *will* and *reason*). Rather, what he means is that our *practice* – our moral experience – testifies to our acknowledgement that pure reason can exercise causality with respect to actions and, hence, that we possess freedom of the will; for, whether we obey the moral law or not, we unquestionably recognize its overriding authority on our actions. But this very acceptance itself shows us that we must acknowledge that we can will freely, since freedom of the will is the condition for the moral law applying to us. Such a justification for ascribing freedom to ourselves *rests* on our practice – on our recognition of the supreme authority of the moral law. It is a practical, not a theoretical proof of our freedom.

So while Kant does not think that he can prove, by means of *theoretical* reason, that we are free, he does nonetheless think that, from a practical point of view, we must acknowledge that we are. The following passage sums up both the centrality of freedom in Kant's moral theory and, at the same time, his conviction that, while we must presuppose it, if we are to be conscious of the authority of the moral law, we cannot prove that we are free on theoretical grounds:

> We have at last traced the determinate concept of morality back to the idea of freedom, but we have been quite unable to demonstrate freedom as something actual in ourselves and in human nature: we saw merely that we must presuppose it if we wish to conceive a being as rational and as endowed with consciousness of his causality in regard to actions – that is, as endowed with a will.
>
> (G, Sect. III: 4:448–9)

Although this quotation comes before Kant introduces – for the *Groundwork* – his distinction between the phenomenal and noumenal worlds, its introduction in no way challenges his conclusion: the conclusion, namely, that although we are unable to prove on theoretical grounds that we are free, we can and must presuppose that we are. For, as he makes clear, while our theoretical reason is unable to¹ provide any proof, it can at least establish – precisely by introducing the phenomena/noumena distinction – that it is *logically possible* that we possess freedom of the will, despite the thoroughgoing determinism in the spatio-temporal (phenomenal) world. Accordingly, there can be no objection, on theoretical grounds, to our moral consciousness providing us with a proof, a practical proof, that we really are free, i.e. by means of our manifest acknowledgement of the supreme authority of the moral law.

(Some writers have urged that, in Section III of the *Groundwork*, there *is* an attempt to provide a theoretical proof of our freedom, and that it is only in the *Critique of Practical Reason* that Kant drops this attempt, replacing it with a practical proof. I reject this reading. As I see it, Kant employs, and only employs, a practical proof of our freedom in *both* texts, viz. by arguing from our consciousness of the authority of the moral law to its necessary presupposition, transcendental freedom. This is the line that I have been developing. I regard the textual evidence in favour of the alternative reading as thin, at best, and the textual evidence against it as very strong. In fact, in summing

up his whole argument, he twice reiterates that freedom is only
a necessary presupposition for those who are conscious that
reason can be practical of itself: see *G*, Sect. III; 5:459 and 461.
Furthermore, given the position that is consistently adopted
throughout the Dialectic of the *Critique of Pure Reason*, namely
that theoretical reason can prove nothing determinate about
the noumenal world, including anything about transcendental
freedom – a view unambiguously repeated in the *Critique of
Practical Reason* – it seems most unlikely that, while sticking
with his noumena/phenomena distinction, Kant could ever have
supposed that a theoretical proof of transcendental freedom was
on the cards).

# The extreme limit of practical philosophy

While we can explain how freedom of the will is logically
possible despite the thoroughgoing determinism in the spatio-
temporal world, and while we can show that in so far as
we credit ourselves with possessing a will, we must think of
ourselves as actually free, we have not thereby explained how the
moral law is able to make the overriding demand upon us that
it actually does. By simply employing our reason with relation
to the moral law, we recognize that, whatever our desires and
inclinations may favour, we *ought* to act only on those maxims
that can stand as universal laws. How can this mere operation of
reason provide us with an overriding motivational authority to
obey the moral law?

Let us be clear: Kant is not in any doubt that we *do* accept the
moral law as giving us an overriding reason for acting. He is not
in the position of an amoralist who, in asking the question 'Why
should I be moral?', is asking for some convincing grounds for
acknowledging the demands of morality even when they clash,
or at least appear to clash, with the objects of his (self-interested)
desires and inclinations. Kant takes it as a *datum* that we do
recognize the necessity of obeying the moral law, of acting for the
sake of duty, however detrimental to our self-interest. His question
concerns *how* such a state of affairs is possible.

Of course, he has, by this stage, already identified the conditions which *allow* us to recognize the supreme authority of the moral law. As members of both the phenomenal and noumenal realms, we are subject to two types of motivation. On the one hand, as members of the phenomenal world (as sensuous beings), we are subject to motivation by desires and inclinations; and if these were the only motivating influences on us, all our actions would be performed for the purpose of maximizing our own happiness (so far at least as we act rationally). On the other hand, as members of the noumenal world (as wholly rational beings), we are subject to motivation by reason alone; and if this were the only motivating influence on us, all our actions would be performed only in so far as our maxims fall under the moral law.

Furthermore, while in our nature as sensuous beings we inevitably have desires and inclinations, in our nature as members of the noumenal world (as rational beings with a will), it is undoubtedly a fact that we recognize that motivation by these sensuous impulses must, on every occasion, give way to motivation by the moral law. In other words, as members of the noumenal world who are nonetheless subject to sensuous impulses, we do recognize the moral law as placing an overriding obligation upon us: that is why, for us, the moral law is conceived as a categorical *imperative*, and the particular principles that the law furnishes are experienced by us as *duties*. For a will – like God's – that is not subject to desires or inclinations, the moral law is never experienced as an imperative. Such a will, 'a holy will', always acts only on the moral law. But our will is, before anything else, subject to determination by sensuous impulses; and, therefore, if pure reason can be practical it needs to be able to *restrain* – and, where acts of moral worth actually occur, *overcome* – these sensuous impulses. This action of reason in opposing our sensuous impulses is the source of our recognition that the moral law places an obligation on us, whatever our desires and inclinations may urge. In thinking of ourselves purely as members of the noumenal world, we accept unhesitatingly that the law governing our actions is the moral law; but because we are also subject to desires and inclinations, we are conscious of this law as putting a *constraint* upon us and that, as members of the noumenal world (as well as the phenomenal world), we *ought* to obey the moral law rather than be motivated by our desires and inclinations.

But while we can, to this extent, explain why as members of both the phenomenal and noumenal worlds we experience the moral law as obliging us to act, we have not thereby explained how reason alone – in determining whether our maxims can stand as universal laws – is *able* to influence the will in opposition to our desires and inclinations. When reason does oppose our sensuous nature, we become conscious of the feeling of respect for the moral law and recognize the overriding necessity of acting for the sake of that law. (In fact, this feeling of respect is one and the same as our recognition of the supreme authority of the moral law). But that is not to explain how reason alone can oppose our sensuous nature by its reflection on the moral law: that we are conscious of this feeling of respect, and that it comes from the exercise of reason opposing our desires and inclinations is – Kant holds – beyond doubt. Yet the question remains: *How* is it possible for the mere exercise of reason to oppose our sensuous nature and give rise to the consciousness of an obligation which, we acknowledge, overrides all other incentives, however useful or immediately pleasurable the attainment of their objects may be?

He believes that we cannot answer this question. And the reason is that, with regard to adequately explaining our consciousness of obligation, the only type of explanation we can grasp has to refer to some direct or indirect *object* of our desires. But any such explanation would precisely destroy the purity of acting from duty – where, as we have seen, there can be no further end for which the action is performed or even any immediate feeling of pleasure as the motivating factor. (Note that the feeling of respect is *not* an immediate feeling. On the contrary, it results *from* the motivating force of pure reason on our desires and inclinations; it is pure reason that provides the initial impetus). Accordingly, the very nature of acting from duty *precludes* our giving any explanation of how reason alone – pure reason – can motivate our sensuously affected will. It is just an ultimate *fact of reason* that, when we submit our maxims to the moral law, we do recognize the necessity of acting for the sake of duty and, hence, that reason alone is able to motivate our will (see *CPractR*, 5:31). To attempt any explanation of reason's motivational capacity would precisely require us to refer to what must negate the *un*conditional nature of the categorical imperative, converting it into a hypothetical imperative: the required autonomy of the will would have been changed into heteronomy of the will, and no action could be conceived as having any moral worth. Of course, we would not, following this conversion, have explained how pure reason can *oppose* any of our sensuous impulses; for once the categorical imperative is changed into a hypothetical one, reason is not motivating the will, but merely deciding on the best means to some desired end.

We have reached the extreme limit of what we can explain, or be expected to explain, with regard to our recognition of the moral law as the supreme principle of action. For while we can set out the preconditions for acting from duty and explain how they can be met (by bringing in the independently justified distinction between the phenomenal and noumenal worlds), we cannot explain how the exercise of reason alone can oppose our sensuous nature and, thereby, instil in us – in the form of the feeling of respect – the recognition of the overriding obligation to obey the moral law:

> But *how* pure reason can be practical in itself without further motives drawn from some other source; that is, how the bare principle of the universal validity of all its maxims as laws ... can by itself – without any matter or object of the will in which we could take some antecedent interest – supply a motive and create an interest which could be called purely moral ... all human reason is totally incapable of explaining, and all the effort and labour to seek such an explanation is wasted.
>
> *(G, Sect. III: 4:461; italics original)*

Nonetheless, the fact remains that pure reason *does* show us that we ought to do our duty whatever our sensuous impulses may urge – or so, at least, Kant has consistently claimed. That the categorical imperative makes this overriding demand upon each of us is a synthetic a priori proposition. It does not follow from the concept of *the will* that an agent *ought* only to act on those maxims that he can will as universal laws. So the proposition is synthetic, not analytic. And, yet, we do recognize its supreme necessity. Hence the proposition must be a priori (since no judgement that carries necessity with it can be derived from experience). But, *unlike* the synthetic a priori propositions of mathematics and pure natural science (dealt with in Part I), there is nothing on the basis of which we can establish this synthetic a priori proposition. It is an ultimate fact, made known to us by our pure practical reason, that we do assent to the proposition that we ought always to accept the moral law as the supreme principle of our action.

Hume had famously questioned the possibility of deducing an *ought* judgement from any *is* judgements, and had argued that unless an explanation can be given of *how* this is possible, all rationalist systems of ethics should be rejected. Kant has replied to this attempt to undermine ethical rationalism by accepting the impossibility of providing any adequate explanation of how reason alone can give rise to our recognition of a moral *ought* judgement, but denying that this subverts his own version of ethical rationalism. From the fact that no such explanation can be given – especially when we can both understand *why* this is so and show that there is *no contradiction* in claiming that pure reason can be practical – it would be premature to reject the capacity of reason alone actually to motivate the will. When it is further admitted that our practice clearly testifies to our acknowledgement that we do possess the capacity to will actions – and, hence, that reason alone really can be practical – we can justifiably maintain that Hume's case for rejecting or subverting any version of ethical rationalism has not been made out.

If it is a fact of reason that merely seeing whether one's maxims can be willed as universal laws does give rise to our recognition of an overriding obligation to duty – and Kant has argued that it does – then it is pointless to seek to reject the capacity of reason alone actually to be practical on the grounds that we cannot see how to justify or explain, on theoretical grounds, any ability of this kind. 'For if as pure reason it is actually practical, it proves its reality and that of its concepts by what it does, and all subtle reasoning against the possibility of its being practical is futile' (*CPractR*, Preface: 5:3).

# The significance of Kant's ethical rationalism

Before we end the chapter, I believe that we can gain a deeper appreciation of Kant's moral system if we can understand why he views the differences between his ethical rationalism and any version of ethical empiricism as profoundly important for our moral practice. That he does so is plain enough; and yet if one stays at the level of observable behaviour, it might at first sight appear a matter of small moment whether one accepts a sophisticated version of ethical empiricism – Hume's theory, for example – or Kant's ethical rationalism. After all, it is not as though there is *in general* a huge gulf in what Hume and Kant would have recommended as the morally right thing to do. Both, for instance, would have recommended relieving those in distress when in a position to do so, of eschewing cruelty, and so on. In short, the *objects* of our moral obligations would be, for the most part, agreed upon by both philosophers.

Why, then, is Kant so opposed to ethical empiricism? There are, I think, two main reasons:

1. The first reason goes back to his contrast between acting from duty and acting from desires and inclinations. Remember that for the ethical empiricist actions can only result from desires or inclinations. Now, as we saw, Kant regards all desires and inclinations as grounded in self-love or one's own happiness; that is, in the pleasures (and avoidance of pains) that the corresponding actions will bring, or are thought to bring, to the agent. If his view is accepted, it follows that, on the empiricist conception, all actions – even those that are wholly in conformity with morality – are, in reality, motivated by self-love, and no action can be performed for the sake of duty, as Kant has analysed our concept of *duty*. He contends, in consequence, that the empiricists' failure to make a sharp distinction – as his own ethics does – between acting from duty and acting from self-love would, if it came into general currency, destroy the *purity* of morality. And this, in turn, would lead to all kinds of special pleading in favour of 'the dear self', whenever there is a clash between the demands of duty and the call of self-interest. If it became generally conceded that duty is nothing more than refined self-love, Kant believes that the line between the two would become increasingly blurred – and to the advantage of our self-love. On this way of viewing the matter, however much the proponents of ethical empiricism may recommend (and with the greatest sincerity) the same or nearly the same duties as Kant, the net effect of basing moral obligation on self-love would, once it become widely disseminated, have an extremely deleterious effect on our moral consciousness. Our sense of the true dignity of morality, which we become aware of by means of the feeling of respect ('which demolishes my self-love'), would certainly be weakened, if not actually destroyed:

Man feels in himself a powerful counterweight to all the
commands of duty ... the counterweight of all his needs and
inclinations, whose total satisfaction he grasps under the name
of 'happiness'. But reason, without promising anything to inclination, enjoins its commands relentlessly, and therefore, so
to speak, with disregard and neglect of these turbulent and
seemingly equitable claims (which refuse to be suppressed by
any command). From this there arises ... a disposition to quibble
with these strict laws of duty, to throw doubt on their validity or
at least on their purity and strictness, and to make them, where
possible, more adapted to our wishes and inclinations; that is, to
pervert their very foundations and destroy their whole dignity –
a result which in the end even ordinary human reason is unable
to approve.

(G, *Section I: 4:405) [see also* G, *Section II: 4:410–12]*

Needless to say, Kant's claim that all desires and inclinations
are prompted solely by self-love has not gone unchallenged.
Following the work of Joseph Butler in his *Fifteen Sermons*,
many philosophers, especially in the ethical empiricist camp,
have held that we possess genuine altruistic desires as well as
purely self-interested or self-regarding ones. Hume is among them.
Following Butler's lead, he points out that while it is frequently the
case that acting benevolently does result in feelings of pleasure to
the agent, and that these (self-regarding) sentiments may become a
*secondary* motive to further acts of benevolence, it is implausible to
claim that all our desires and inclinations are, in the first instance,
initiated by self-love. Unless we felt an immediate desire or aversion
to certain objects, i.e. prior to any consideration of self-love, we
would have very few desires at all; for we require an original
tendency towards certain objects in order to experience pleasure in
their fulfilment. Moreover, given the general behaviour of human
beings, it is, in fact, reasonable to maintain that benevolence is
among those inclinations that we do immediately and frequently
feel towards certain of our fellow creatures. It is, in other words,
reasonable to hold that it is a genuinely altruistic passion or
inclination, not one dependent on self-love, even if some acts of
benevolence do have self-love as a secondary motive:

Were there no appetite of any kind antecedent to self-love, that propensity would scarcely ever exert itself; because we should, in that case, have felt few and slender pains and pleasures ... Now where is the difficulty in conceiving that this may likewise be the case with benevolence and friendship that, from the original frame of our temper, we may feel a desire of another's happiness or good, which, by means of that affection, becomes our own good, and is afterwards pursued, from the combined motives of benevolence and self-enjoyment?

(An Enquiry concerning the Principles of Morals, *Appendix II* '*Of self-love*')

Plainly, if this alternative view is correct, Kant's first main reason for opposing any version of ethical empiricism is thrown into question. It is sometimes said in Kant's defence that his deepest reason for opposing duty to desires and inclinations is not that the latter are grounded in self-love (as, it is admitted, he does maintain), but that whereas the laws of duty apply to all *possible* finite rational creatures, there are *no* particular desires or inclinations which will be common to every such being. Hence, even if Kant is mistaken in holding that desires and inclinations are invariably grounded in self-love, his essential point will remain, viz. that no moral obligations can be based on desires and inclinations. For if the basic demands of morality hold for all possible finite rational beings with a will, it follows that, since no particular desires or inclinations (including altruistic ones) are shared by all of them, morality cannot be founded on any desires or inclinations.

While it is manifestly correct to affirm that Kant believes that moral obligation applies to all possible (finite) agents, not just human ones, it is less clear that this is essentially the point he is driving out in opposing duty to self-love. Certainly, if, like Kant, you hold that all desires and inclinations are grounded in self-love and, at the same time, you hold that we oppose duty to self-love (as most ethical empiricists would accept), it will be a *consequence* of this position that morality cannot be founded on any desires or inclinations and must, instead, be founded on reason alone. For, once desires and inclinations are discounted because they are grounded in self-love, reason will be the only thing that finite rational beings can have in common. But this route to showing that any viable ethical system must be based on pure reason, and not on any desires or inclinations, precisely depends on holding that self-love grounds all our desires and inclinations. It does not provide an argument for claiming that Kant's primary motive for throwing out desires and inclinations, as an acceptable basis for our concept of *duty* or *moral obligation*, is that no particular sensuous impulses are shared by all possible finite rational beings with a will.

However, even if it were true that Kant opposes a moral system based on desires and inclinations primarily because no such system could apply to every possible finite agent, this is unlikely to cut much ice with ethical empiricists. They would probably reply that if there are altruistic desires which virtually all humans share (to some degree), the fact that a moral system which is based on them cannot necessarily hold for all *other* finite agents is of little or no consequence. Our moral obligations are addressed to human beings, and we should not worry if they cannot also be justifiably applied to every other finite rational being with a will, provided that *we* have a working system that opposes moral obligation to self-love.

There is more to be said on this issue, on both sides, but I will leave the discussion here.

2. The second main reason for Kant's rejection of ethical empiricism is his belief that it entirely knocks away the fundamental condition for morality to exist at all. This condition is freedom of the will.

Even allowing that there are altruistic desires and inclinations as well as those deriving from self-love, this second reason for rejecting ethical empiricism evidently remains to be answered. It is Kant's deepest and most wide-ranging objection to the empiricist alternative. We have seen from the discussion of transcendental freedom in the *Critique of Pure Reason* that he regards it as conclusively proved that desires and inclinations are invariably causally determined by earlier factors in the temporal series of events (and these events in turn are causally determined by still earlier ones and so on). Consequently, if the *only* possible motivational factors are desires and inclinations – as an ethical empiricist maintains – it follows that an agent can never exercise his will freely, given Kant's requirement that such freedom depends on an agent's capacity to will an action *on the basis of reason alone*. Moreover, we have seen that Kant regards the exercise of reason as operating altogether *outside* the causally determined temporal realm – in the noumenal world – and, hence, as not subject, as are all desires and inclinations (whether altruistic or self-regarding), to the causality of nature. Accordingly, on his version of ethical rationalism, it is possible for agents to will freely and so to perform morally worthy acts. But, as he sees it, we are totally incapable of any acts of moral consequence on the ethical empiricist picture. On this picture, each of us is merely a cog (or set of cogs) in the vast deterministic spatio-temporal world of events; there can be no question of acts freely performed and so no question of our possessing moral worth. Human beings are reduced to *mere* (conscious) mechanisms, with no intrinsic value: instead of being 'ends in ourselves', we are nothing more than conscious automata bereft of any true dignity. This, at any rate, is how Kant sees the consequences of accepting ethical empiricism; and he regards the effect that such an attitude would have upon us, not least from a moral point of view, as wholly demeaning.

Here again, we see the importance to Kant of his Copernican revolution in metaphysics. Without the distinction between the phenomenal and noumenal worlds, it would be impossible, he holds, to defend morality as a going concern or conceive of ourselves as capable of directing our own ends. But, with that revolution in place, freedom of the will can be proved from a practical point of view, and the dignity of human beings – as moral agents existing outside the determinism of nature – can be justifiably affirmed. Transcendental freedom is 'the *keystone* of the whole structure of a system of pure reason' (*CPractR*, Preface; 5:3–4; italics original). In the next chapter, we shall further discuss his concept of freedom and the way in which he sees it as supporting our right to believe in God and the immortality of the soul. But I hope that we have already gained some better understanding of why Kant regards the differences between his own ethical theory and the empiricist alternative as of considerably more than theoretical interest.

# 6

# The highest good and why it requires the existence of God and the immortality of the soul as well as freedom of the will

One might well have expected that Kant would have ended his exploration of the foundations of morality at the point where he claims to have justified, so far as it is possible, the supreme principle of morals (the moral law or categorical imperative) – which itself includes providing a practical proof of our freedom. These issues were dealt with in the previous two chapters. In fact, this is where he does close down his discussion in the *Groundwork*; and, allowing for a more detailed examination of these matters, it is substantially where he ends the Analytic of Pure Practical

Reason in the *Critique of Practical Reason*. But, in that later work and, more exactly, in the immediately ensuing Dialectic of Pure Practical Reason (5:107–48), Kant argues that the very demands that the categorical imperative impose on us lead to an intractable contradiction unless we delve still further into the *metaphysical* foundations of morality.

On the issues surrounding these metaphysical foundations, I recommend, as extremely helpful additional reading, the concluding Appendix of the *Critique of Judgement*, entitled Methodology of the Teleological Judgement, notably sections 86–91 (5:442–84). These sections – including the General Remark on Teleology – cast considerable light on the matters discussed in the Dialectic of Pure Practical Reason but are, sadly, rarely studied at least in this context.

# The antinomy of pure practical reason

In the *Critique of Pure Reason*, Kant had argued that questions concerning the existence of three 'objects' – God, freedom and immortality – form the core of speculative metaphysics; but he had further argued that it is quite impossible for theoretical reason to prove or disprove the existence of any of them. Now we saw, in the previous chapter, that so far as freedom of the will is concerned, it is our recognition of the validity of the moral law – that this law has supreme authority over our actions – which shows us that we must acknowledge that we really are free, i.e. that it is not only *logically possible* for our will to be free, despite the determinism of nature, but that we actually possess that capacity. The proof of our freedom, then, is not accomplished by theoretical reason but by practical reason. More particularly, by what Kant calls, in the *Critique of Practical Reason*, 'the fact of reason', viz. by our immediate recognition of the validity of the moral law whenever we draw up a maxim for our actions. For if we really do recognize, as a fact given to us by practical reason, that the moral law has supreme authority over our wills then we can equally know that we possess freedom of the will. As Kant puts it:

> But among all the ideas of speculative reason freedom is also the only one the possibility of which we *know* a priori, though

without having insight into it, because it is the condition of the moral law, which we do know ... practical reason of itself, without any collusion with speculative reason, furnishes reality to a supersensible object of the category of causality, namely to freedom (although, as a practical concept, only for practical use), and hence establishes by means of a fact what could there [*i.e.* in the *Critique of Pure Reason*] only be thought.

(CPractR, *5:4–6; italics original*)

What of the other two central ideas of speculative metaphysics: *God* and *the immortality of the soul*? At first sight, it would seem unlikely that practical reason could provide any justified grounds for believing in their existence. It would seem unlikely because of Kant's insistence that only a purely *formal* principle, namely the moral law or categorical imperative, can provide the motivation for acts of moral worth. No thought either about the majesty and power of a (possible) God or about a (possible) hereafter can be allowed to enter into one's grounds for doing what is morally obligatory. Yet, in the Dialectic of Pure Practical Reason, Kant does argue that the existence of God and the immortality of the soul are *also* necessary for us to think of the moral law or categorical imperative as the supreme principle of all our actions.

How does this come about? It comes about because, having shown that the categorical imperative is the overriding law of action, and that we are, accordingly, required to act for the sake of duty whenever the occasion demands it, we find that there is an apparent conflict (or antinomy) in our thinking about the moral life. For while it is undoubtedly the *first* and *supreme* condition upon us to become perfectly virtuous – that is, to cultivate a moral disposition to act dutifully whenever occasion demands it – it is *also* the case that, as finite rational beings, we need happiness in order to be fulfilled. Consequently, although the cultivation of the moral disposition is the primary condition governing us (and the *sine qua non* of our right to obtain the happiness that we desire), it is not what Kant calls our highest good (the *summum bonum*). Our highest good is the *union* – the necessary connection – of perfect virtuousness and commensurate happiness. By making ourselves *worthy* to be happy – through the cultivation of the moral disposition (itself required by the moral law) – reason requires that, as a consequence, we participate in the happiness which we need as finite rational beings:

> To need happiness, to be worthy of it [by making ourselves fully virtuous], and yet not to participate in it cannot be consistent with the perfect volition of a rational being that has all power (even if we think of such a being by way of experiment only).
> (CPractR, 5:110)

Put briefly, there are two conditions that need to be fulfilled if finite rational beings are to obtain their highest good: these beings are required to make themselves perfectly virtuous and, as a consequence, obtain happiness proportionate to their virtue. Their constitution as sensuous as well as rational beings entails that it is *necessary* for them to receive happiness commensurate with their virtue: this is a judgement which, Kant holds, any perfectly rational being would make. However, if the highest good, the union of complete virtuousness with commensurate happiness, is not even in principle achievable, it follows that there is a contradiction in our thinking. As finite rational beings, we acknowledge that we are obliged (by the moral law) to make ourselves worthy to be happy by means of the cultivation of the moral disposition. But if it is provable that the highest good cannot be achieved as the necessary consequence of this cultivation, it follows that the moral law is requiring a result (the union of perfect virtuousness with commensurate happiness) which it cannot consistently require – because its achievement is unattainable. Since this impossible requirement results from the demands of the moral law, it follows that this fundamental law of morality must itself be rejected.

But why should it be supposed impossible for us to achieve the highest good? The answer is that since (as we have seen from the previous two chapters) the pursuit of duty and that of own happiness are two distinct activities, it cannot follow, as a matter of definition, that if each person makes himself perfectly virtuous, commensurate happiness must result, i.e. it is not an *analytic* truth that the first requisite of the highest good (the acquisition of the moral disposition) entails the second (commensurate happiness), or vice versa. But, in which case, how can the necessary synthesis of virtue and happiness come about, so that the highest good is achieved?

At best, only two ways are conceivable: either the desire for happiness must produce the moral disposition or the moral disposition must produce happiness. The first of these alternatives can be swiftly rejected: no acts which result solely from the desire for happiness can have any moral worth, however much the actions produced may *conform* to the dictates of the moral law. Virtuous conduct requires that the action is performed *for the sake of* the moral law, and not from the desire for happiness. The trouble is that the other alternative also appears equally unacceptable, viz. that the cultivation of the moral disposition will necessarily result in commensurate happiness. It looks as if it could only be a matter of *chance* that the two should be coordinate: for the satisfaction of a finite being's need for happiness depends upon the contingencies of the natural world (and these are never completely under the control of finite beings). Hence, it seems that there can be no grounds whatever for supposing that perfect virtuousness and commensurate happiness will be necessarily connected. On the face of it, therefore, the moral antinomy is irresolvable: it is, it appears, impossible for the required connection of virtue with happiness to take place. Consequently, the moral law itself – which generates this contradictory requirement – must be declared a self-contradictory principle.

Kant sees only one way in which we can resolve the antinomy. This is to have recourse to the distinction between the phenomenal and noumenal worlds: a distinction which he has already appealed to, in his moral philosophy, in order to prove (as he claims) that we really are capable of exercising our wills freely. If we now assume the existence, in the noumenal world, of an intelligent moral author of nature (the phenomenal world), we can allow that nature, including its laws, has been intentionally created so that the highest good can be achieved with certainty by each of us. The cause of nature needs to be thought of as acting on the basis of understanding (or intelligence) and will (or intention) because only in this way can we conceive of the creator as capable of assessing our worthiness to be happy and constructing an order of nature that necessarily leads to the highest good. 'Therefore the supreme cause of nature, in so far as it must be presupposed for the highest good, is a being that is the cause of nature by *understanding* and *will* (hence its author), that is *God*' (CPractR, 5:125; italics original).

Moreover, since the achievement of the highest good requires that we make ourselves *fully* virtuous – that we acquire a disposition which, on all possible occasions, performs what is morally enjoined (the moral disposition) – we must also presuppose the immortality of the soul. For, as beings subject to temptation from sensuous impulses, the acquisition of the moral disposition requires an *endless progress* on our part to that state in which we can never be motivated by any sensuous impulse and always act for the sake of the moral law. 'This endless progress,' Kant says, 'is however possible only on the presupposition of the *existence* and personality of the same rational being continuing *endlessly* (which is called the immortality of the soul)' (*CPractR*, 5:122; italics original).

The existence of God and the immortality (or permanence) of the soul are, together, the two presuppositions which can alone resolve the moral antinomy for us. Kant calls them 'postulates of pure practical reason'. A postulate of pure practical reason refers to the existence of a possible object – understood to include a state or capacity – which, while it cannot be proved to exist by theoretical reason, is nonetheless inseparably connected with the moral law; and so, given our recognition of the unconditional validity of that law, must be presupposed by us.

That our will is capable of acting freely has already been shown to be necessary for the moral law to apply to us, even though its existence cannot be proved (or disproved) by theoretical reason. So there are, in fact, *three* postulates of pure practical reason, those referring respectively to God, freedom and immortality. But there is this difference at least: whereas freedom of the will is the sole condition for our being subject to the moral law, the existence of God and the immortality of the soul are conditions that need to be added in order for us to be able to realize the object of the moral law, the highest good. Obedience to the moral law alone remains the *determining ground* for our acting in each and every case: from the moral point of view, we must not introduce the thought of future happiness as a motive for steadfastly complying with what duty commands. While we act for the sake of duty, we are making ourselves *worthy to be happy*; but if we act in order to receive commensurate happiness in the future, we act heteronomously and our action has, to that extent, no moral worth. In short, while the object of the moral law, the final end of all our moral endeavours, is the *union* of perfect virtuousness (the moral disposition) with commensurate happiness or, in other words, the highest good, the determining ground of all our actions, in so far as they can have any moral worth, must be obedience to the moral law alone.

The relation between the ground and object of the moral law raises the intriguing question of whether, on the Kantian moral system, an atheist can lead an entirely morally worthy life. While Kant consistently argues that an atheist cannot *absolve* himself from obedience to the moral law (since, as we have just noted, neither immortality nor God's existence is required for the moral law to apply to us in any individual case), there remains the issue of whether an atheist can have an unwavering commitment to the moral life. In the *Critique of Judgement*, Spinoza is offered as an example of someone who strove to be morally upright while, at the same time, denying the existence of God and the immortality of the soul. As Kant sees it, such an atheist, if fully rational, must find himself in a psychologically unsatisfactory state. It is, after all, one's commitment to the moral law that *leads* to the postulation of the immortality of the soul and the existence of God, i.e. in order wholly to comply with the demands of the moral law (the acquisition of the moral disposition) and to make possible its rationally necessary consequence (happiness commensurate with perfect virtue). A morally committed atheist must find himself in the unfortunate position of someone who is striving continually to act for the sake of duty while, yet, repudiating the conditions that make the object of the moral law, the highest good, possible (not only for himself but for all finite rational beings). No atheist, Kant claims, can both fully accept the demands of the moral law and simultaneously refuse to acknowledge its required consequence, the highest good in the world. Without both the immortality of the soul and the existence of God, it is impossible for us to conceive of the necessary accomplishment of this end; and so it is impossible for us to manifest unwavering or wholehearted acceptance of the moral law (which commands its fulfilment). Accordingly, if the atheist is to commit himself fully to the requirements laid down by the moral law 'he must assume the existence of a *moral* author of the world, that is, of a God. As this assumption at least involves nothing intrinsically self-contradictory he may quite readily make it ... at least for the purpose of framing a conception of the possibility of the final end morally prescribed to him' (*Critique of Judgement*: Sect. 87; 5:450–3; italics original). The atheist cannot be satisfied with the possible chance concurrence of the moral disposition with commensurate happiness because the moral law – which he himself accepts – makes it *necessary* that they are coordinate; and such a connection can be conceived by us only through postulating a moral author of the world.

# Have the demands of morality extended our knowledge beyond the sensible world?

The three postulates of pure practical reason are described as 'morally necessary', and they are said to give 'objective reality' to our ideas of *God*, *freedom* and *immortality*.

But how can Kant maintain the objective reality of these ideas, given that the *Critique of Pure Reason* has declared that it is completely impossible for us to tell, by means of pure (theoretical) reason, whether any of the ideas of transcendent metaphysics – and, more especially, those of *God*, *freedom* and *immortality* – have real objects corresponding to them? It would seem that he has gone right back on one of the chief results of that earlier *Critique*, namely, that without sensible intuition, we cannot acquire any determinate theoretical knowledge whatsoever – and, hence, none concerning what may exist in the noumenal world.

Kant's answer to this concern is not straightforward, and it will, in the end, require a separation between our idea of *freedom of the will*, on the one hand, and those of *God* and *immortality*, on the other. But, at the outset, the Dialectic places all three ideas on the same footing with respect to our right to affirm their objective reality. I shall first outline this initial strategy, before explaining why Kant does finally separate them into two groups.

Given that these three ideas are necessarily related to our recognition of the moral law (as a self-consistent principle), we are entitled to affirm their objective reality because, in doing so, we are not making any theoretical claim about the *character* of these objects. Sensible intuition would indeed be required to do this. Admittedly, pure practical reason, through its demand that we seek to realize the highest good, *has* extended our theoretical knowledge beyond what can be achieved by theoretical reason. But this knowledge concerns only the reality – the *existence* – of God, freedom and immortality; nothing is thereby learned concerning their attributes, at least so far as it increases our theoretical knowledge of these objects. While we may be able to characterize, to determine, these objects *for moral purposes*, we can tell nothing about how these attributes can be employed *outside* the moral sphere. For instance, Kant does undoubtedly think that, for moral purposes, we can determine more precisely the character of God: he thinks that we can tell (at least) that He must be omniscient, omnipotent, omnipresent and eternal (*CPractR*, 5:140). These attributes are held to be required in order for God to comprehend exactly the moral character of every finite rational being, both now and in the endless future, and to arrange, in each case, a precisely fitting connection between the virtuousness that each attains and commensurate happiness. But he is adamant that whatever capacity we may have to determine the attributes of these objects for practical purposes, this cannot enable us to gain any *theoretical* knowledge about them or use them to extend our theoretical knowledge of the sensible world:

> Thus by the practical law that commands the existence of the highest good possible in the world, the possibility of those objects of pure speculative reason, the objective reality of which the latter could not assure them, is postulated; by this the theoretical cognition of pure reason certainly receives an increment, but it consists only in this: that those concepts [*God, freedom* and *immortality*] otherwise problematic (merely thinkable) for it, are now declared assertorically to be concepts to which real objects belong, because practical reason unavoidably requires the existence of them for the possibility of its object, the highest good, which is absolutely necessary practically, and theoretical reason is therefore justified in assuming them. But this extension of theoretical reason is no extension of speculation, that is, no possible use can now be made of it *for theoretical purposes*.
>
> *(CPractR, 5:134; italics original)*

\*

I said earlier that Kant does not, in the end, treat *freedom of the will* on exactly the same footing as the other two ideas of pure practical reason. While he continues to assert that we can indeed *know* that we are free, it turns out that he does *not* think that our right to affirm the objective reality of God and the immortality of the soul does amount to our knowing that they exist. It would be a mistake, however, to suppose that the grounds for this discrimination arises merely from the following difference: whereas freedom of the will is a presupposition of the moral law applying to us at all, the existence of God and the soul's immortality are only presuppositions of our realizing the end to which the moral law directs us, viz. the highest good. By itself, this difference is insufficient to justify withholding a claim to knowledge with respect to the latter ideas (*God* and *immortality*), while allowing it with respect to the former (*freedom*). It is insufficient because all three ideas, as Kant has so far represented them, are *required* for the moral law to be a genuinely self-consistent principle: without the postulation of all three ideas, it looks as though the moral law, together with its inevitable consequence, cannot be coherently thought. So, given our recognition of the supreme authority of the moral law, why does Kant deny that our right to affirm the objective reality of the latter two ideas can amount to our knowledge of their existence, while he sticks to his claim that we do have knowledge of the former idea?

The reason is that despite all that he has said about the requirement to postulate the existence of God and the immortality of the soul in order for the highest good to be attained, it transpires that this requirement is only a *subjective* one. That is, although *we* cannot see how the object of the moral law – the highest good – can be achieved without the existence of God and the immortality of the soul, it is not provably impossible that this object should be attained without their existence. The most that we are entitled to assert is that it is impossible *for us* to understand how there could be the required connection between virtue and happiness without the existence of God and the soul's immortality. Given our faculty of understanding, we cannot grasp how the union of the moral disposition and commensurate happiness could be achieved unless there exists *an intelligent moral author* of the spatio-temporal world, i.e. a cause of the world that will bring about the necessary harmony between the moral law and the (very different) laws of nature through *understanding* and *will*. But this failure of comprehension on our part is not a strict proof that it is absolutely impossible for this union to be achieved through a cause which acts *without* understanding and will, and so *without* the need to postulate an intelligent author of the world (God).

Since, as Kant holds, we can only grasp how the required union of virtue and happiness is possible by postulating the being of a God as well as the soul's immortality, it is subjectively necessary for us to assume their existence. After all, our recognition of the validity of the moral law does require us to think of its object, the highest good, as attainable (otherwise we would be involved in self-contradiction). And since we can only think of the highest good as attainable by postulating God's existence and the immortality of the soul, it is morally necessary that we do postulate them. Kant's position is that we are *justified* in assuming their existence on moral grounds (given the ideas are theoretically possible ones), although this justification cannot amount to *knowledge* of their reality. He calls the assumption of God's existence, together with the accompanying assumption of the soul's immortality, '*a pure practical rational belief*' (CPractR, 5:146; italics original). This is what he elsewhere refers to, somewhat misleadingly, as a matter of 'faith'. Thus, when he famously says, in the second preface to the *Critique of Pure Reason*, 'I have therefore found it necessary to deny *knowledge*, in order to make room for *faith*' (B xxx; italics original), he does not mean that we can only have an *unsupported* commitment to God's existence and the soul's immortality. On the contrary, he thinks that the objective reality of both the idea of *God* and that of *immortality* are, from our point of view, entirely justified on moral grounds. Nonetheless, we cannot declare it to be objectively necessary to presuppose the existence of God and the soul's immortality because it is not provably impossible for the highest good to be achievable without their presupposition.

What, then, of the third of the ideas of pure practical reason, *freedom of the will*? Why does Kant maintain that, in the case of this idea, we can know that it has objective reality? The answer is that since each of us has immediate moral experience of the supreme authority of the moral law (in the feeling of respect) and since this experience is only possible on the presupposition that we can will freely, we can know that the idea of freedom must have objective reality. This idea is the only one of the three ideas of pure practical reason that we can know for certain really exists. That is why Kant calls it the '*keystone*' of the whole of speculative reason. It alone provides us with some determinate knowledge of the noumenal world (though only for practical purposes); and through it we are able to have pure practical rational belief in God and immortality.

But note that the proof of our freedom is not accomplished by theoretical reason: it is accomplished by practical reason. So the claim, originally made in the *Critique of Pure Reason*, that pure (theoretical) reason is unable to prove anything about the noumenal world remains in force; the increment in our knowledge of the transcendent has been achieved by practical reason. Nonetheless, by the time of the *Critique of Practical Reason*, Kant no longer thought that the reality of freedom – like that of God or the immortality of the soul – is only a matter of faith (or pure practical rational belief). Of the three central ideas of speculative metaphysics, it alone can be known to have objective reality (and its law determined) – though not by means of theoretical reason but by means of our moral experience (our recognition of the supreme authority of the moral law), and so by means of pure *practical* reason.

# Freedom of the will: a secure keystone for the system of pure reason?

Any application of the moral law to us depends on the existence of freedom of the will. For although Kant contends that *knowledge* of our freedom rests on our prior recognition of the supreme authority of the moral law, it is nonetheless the case – as he openly admits – that freedom of our will is necessary for the moral law to apply to us (see *CPractR*, 5:4, footnote).

Given the centrality of freedom to his moral theory and to his system of speculative metaphysics in general, we need further to investigate the plausibility of his defence of transcendental freedom. For it is transcendental freedom which, as Kant sees it, is necessary for the moral law to apply to us: only in so far as an agent can *originate* the decision to act, that is, bring about the decision *without* being determined to do so by earlier events in the temporal series, can the agent possess the freedom required for morality. Both in the Dialectic of the *Critique of Pure Reason* and, again, in the Analytic of the *Critique of Practical Reason*, Kant argues that, given (but only given) the phenomena/noumena distinction, it is logically possible for us to possess transcendental freedom, despite the existence of a thoroughgoing determinism in the spatio-temporal world. I explained his argument for this conclusion in Part I (Chapter 3), without calling into question its success. I followed this strategy because, at the level at which he there defends transcendental freedom, I believe that his defence succeeds. Within the system of transcendental idealism, it is logically possible for all changes in the spatio-temporal world to be subject to natural necessity *and* for an agent to bring about actions in this world through transcendental freedom.

But it is far from clear that given the type of determinism which, on empirical grounds, it would appear reasonable to believe obtains in the spatio-temporal world, we can suppose that transcendental freedom can ever be manifested in nature. The point here is not that, at the subatomic level, there seems to be strong evidence for thinking that there is not thoroughgoing determinism (although this is, indeed, a serious challenge to Kant's theory of knowledge, if subatomic particles are possible objects of our experience). It is rather that, even at the macroscopic level, where we may reasonably assume universal, or virtually universal, determinism – including the causation of desires or inclinations – there looks to be a serious difficulty for Kant's defence of transcendental freedom. In order to explain the difficulty, I will begin by rehearsing the argument for the logical possibility of transcendental freedom; but I will now place that argument squarely within his moral system. As we have found, it is our obligation to act for the sake of the moral law that requires the capacity to will freely.

In the case of a perceived situation of moral consequence, Kant's picture is of an agent who is initially caused, by prior events in the temporal series, to have a particular desire or inclination which would itself produce an action *unless* the noumenal self, on the basis of pure practical reason, overcomes this sensuously produced desire and produces an alternative action, i.e. one that is performed for the sake of duty. The alternative, morally worthy action, is brought about by pure practical reason opposing the sensuously produced desire through instilling an operative feeling of respect in the temporal series of events. (We discussed the relation between desires and inclinations, on the one hand, and the feeling of respect, on the other, in Chapter 4 under 'The feeling of respect'.) On this picture, whether an agent's action is produced by a sensuous desire or by a feeling of respect, there will be no break in the natural necessity that is required in the spatio-temporal world. Clearly, there will be no break in natural necessity where an action results from a sensuously produced desire: this same type and strength of desire is always going to be produced, under the same circumstances, and it will always result, under those circumstances, in the same action (granting, of course, Kant's contention that there exists thoroughgoing natural necessity in the phenomenal world). But, equally, there is going to be no break in the chain of natural necessity where an action is produced by the noumenal self *overcoming* a given sensuously produced desire, thereby instilling a feeling of respect into the agent's consciousness and one which is strong enough to bring about an ensuing (morally worthy) action. Since the noumenal self is an atemporal entity, its choice of action is not going to be subject to change; and so this particular decision, based on pure practical reason's application of the moral law to the agent's maxim, stands for all similar circumstances.

Consequently, whether an agent's action is passively produced through a given desire or actively produced by pure practical reason, there must be a *constant conjunction* between those given surrounding circumstances, on the one hand, and the ensuing action, on the other. So far as concerns the conditions required for ascribing natural necessity to the events of the spatio-temporal world, these will be fulfilled whether the agent acts through a sensuously produced desire or through pure practical reason (via the production of an operative feeling of respect):

> But I say: *the law of nature stands*, whether the rational being is the cause, by reason and through freedom, of effects in the world of the senses, or whether it does not determine these effects out of grounds of reason. For in the first case the act happens according to maxims the effect of which in appearance will always be in conformity with constant laws; in the second case, the act happening not in accordance with principles of reason, it is subject to empirical laws of sensibility [involving desires or inclinations], and in both cases the effects are connected according to constant laws; we demand no more for natural necessity, indeed we know nothing more of it.
>
> *(Prol., Sect. 53; 4:345–6; italics original)*

It is precisely because of this observed regularity between the given surrounding circumstances of an agent and the type of action that ensues – whether the action arises from a sensuous desire or a feeling of respect – that we are enabled to determine the particular empirical character of any given agent; and, then, from knowledge of this character, go on to predict future actions, granting also our knowledge of the agent's surrounding circumstances.

Kant's model seems to me to be a consistent one for admitting the logical possibility of transcendental freedom even within a spatio-temporal world that can legitimately be seen as governed throughout by natural necessity. For, on his model, all that the ascription of natural necessity requires is unbroken regularity in the sequence of appearances. But the application of this logical possibility to our actual spatio-temporal world depends on the assumption that an agent's own grounds for acting on any given occasion, whether this is a naturally produced desire or a noumenally produced feeling of respect, can make a *difference* to the behaviour of the ensuing series of physical events leading to the action. Kant is definitely not taking it that from a mere knowledge of the physical laws and the disposition of the physical events in the universe – let us say 200 years *before* the agent had even been born – all the actions of that agent could, in principle, be predicted with certainty. To the contrary, he is taking it that the occurrence to the agent of a sensuous desire or feeling of respect can alter what would otherwise occur, i.e. on the basis of merely physical laws. To repeat: this assumption, if correct, would not interfere with natural necessity, as Kant understands that notion. It would not, since the occurrence of the same desire or feeling of respect to a given agent would always occur, under the same circumstances, and would invariably be followed by the same action. Admittedly, such an assumption does require that there are more than purely physical causal laws governing what observable actions occur in the spatio-temporal world: an agent's actions are, on this picture, governed by irreducibly mental phenomena (states existing only in time) as well as physical ones. But Kant is undoubtedly allowing, indeed insisting, on such a picture.

The difficulty with the picture is that it appears to be at odds with a consequence of the empirical evidence, viz. that we could in principle infallibly predict all of an agent's observable actions from knowledge of the physical state of the universe any number of years before the agent is born. In other words, given the empirical evidence, there is, it seems, no room for the noumenal self to intervene in the series of events, thereby making possible an action of moral worth by the agent. Accordingly, Kant's contention that, granting the phenomena/noumena distinction, our consciousness that we are bound by the moral law proves the reality (not the mere logical possibility) of our freedom will have to be rejected. Our *alleged* recognition of the supreme authority of the moral law – the so-called 'fact of reason' – will not be a genuine recognition after all or, at least, there would appear to be strong grounds for believing that it is not genuine.

Once knowledge of our freedom has been thus called into question, Kant's argument for a justified belief in both the immortality of the soul and the existence of God can no longer be upheld. For his argument depends on our really being summoned to achieve the highest good. But if we have no transcendental freedom (or at least strong grounds for thinking that we have no such freedom), there can be no good reason for believing we have any such summons. Since the keystone to speculative reason has collapsed, so too does the whole enterprise of Kant's speculative metaphysics.

This does not mean that we can, without more ado, simply embrace instead some sophisticated version of ethical empiricism. For all that has been shown, Kant may be correct in his claim that if morality is not to be an empty delusion, we require his version of ethical rationalism, including the existence of transcendental freedom. He may yet be correct in thinking that freedom of the will, as he conceives it, is too central to our conception of morality to be renounced without bringing down with it any viable notion of ourselves as moral beings. Such a conclusion may indeed be mistaken; but, given the power and depth of Kant's ethics, it will, I think, require a sustained argument to show that this is so.[1]

# ENDNOTE

1 It has been claimed that there is an entirely a priori way of rejecting
  Kant's argument for transcendental freedom. According to this
  objection, Kant *himself* holds that the noumenal subject can only
  possess transcendental freedom if it creates its own noumenal
  character. But, the criticism continues, to suppose that the noumenal
  subject can be a *causa sui* – the entire cause of its own character – is
  incoherent. Therefore, the agent (qua noumenal subject) cannot, as
  Kant supposes, be capable of acting in the phenomenal world through
  transcendental freedom. Hence, it is not a coherent requirement for
  morality to apply to us that we possess transcendental freedom;
  and so there can be no objection, on that score, to our embracing a
  sophisticated version of ethical empiricism.

  There is, in my opinion, no good reason for supposing that Kant
  thinks of the noumenal subject as a *causa sui*: on the contrary, he
  clearly wishes to allow for the possibility that we, as noumenal
  subjects, are creatures, that is, are created by God. But from the
  assumed fact that God has created the noumenal subject, it does
  not follow that it is impossible for an agent to bring about actions
  in the phenomenal world through transcendental freedom. Such a
  consequence would only follow if God (and the noumenal subject)
  existed *in time*. But God has *created* the noumenal subject, i.e. has
  generated its existence through a *non-temporal* act, and, hence, the
  noumenal subject can bring about actions in the phenomenal world
  without being itself determined by anything which precedes it in
  time. When it does so, the actions that appear have arisen from
  transcendental freedom, since the agent's will has produced the actions
  *spontaneously* (on the basis of pure practical reason). Accordingly,
  each action is correctly attributed to the agent as it originated from
  him (qua noumenal subject) and not from God – even though God is
  the creator of the noumenal subject. (These points are well brought
  out in the *Critique of Practical Reason*, see especially 5:100–2.)

  The question as to why the noumenal subject brings about certain
  actions in the world and not others – thereby creating a particular

*empirical* character – is entirely outside our possible knowledge (as Kant explicitly notes: *CPR*, A 557/B 585). However, the fact that God is assumed to have created the noumenal subject fails to show that, *in the sense that Kant intended*, the agent, qua noumenal subject, cannot freely have willed the action or be the one to whom the action is rightly attributed or be the creator (or originator) of the empirical character, whether good or evil.

# BIBLIOGRAPHY

## I Primary texts cited

### Kant's works: a selection of modern translations

When multiple translations of the same text are given, I have quoted from the one marked by an asterisk (apart from minor changes); but all the listed translations are worth consulting.

*Critique of [the Power of] Judgement*, trans. Werner Pluhar (Indianapolis, 1987), Paul Guyer and Eric Matthews (Cambridge, 2000), and J. C. Meredith (revised N. Walker) (Oxford, 2007)*.

*Critique of Practical Reason*, trans. T. K. Abbott, 6th edn (London, 1909), L. W. Beck (Chicago, 1949), Mary Gregor (Cambridge, 1997)*, and Werner Pluhar (Indianapolis, 2002).

*Critique of Pure Reason*, trans. Werner Pluhar (Indianapolis, 1996), Paul Guyer and Allen W. Wood (Cambridge, 1997), and N. K. Smith (Basingstoke, revised 2nd edition, 2007)*.

*Groundwork for [or of]the Metaphysics of Morals*, trans. L. W. Beck, under the title *Foundations of the Metaphysics of Morals* with Critical Essays (ed. Robert P. Wolff) (Indianapolis, 1969), Mary Gregor (Cambridge, 1997), H. J. Paton, originally entitled *The Moral Law* (London, 1964)*, and Arnulf Zweig (Oxford, 2002).

*The Metaphysics of Morals*, trans. Mary Gregor (Cambridge, 1991).

*Practical Philosophy*, trans. Mary Gregor (Cambridge, 1996). Contains the *Critique of Practical Reason*, *Groundwork for the Metaphysics of Morals* and *The Metaphysics of Morals* as well as other ethical writings by Kant.

*Prolegomena to Any Future Metaphysics*, trans. Peter G. Lucas (Manchester, 1953)*, James Ellington (Indianapolis, 1977), and Gary Hatfield (Cambridge, revised edition, 2004).

## Other works: modern editions

Butler, Joseph, *Fifteen Sermons Preached at the Rolls Chapel*, ed. T. A. Roberts (London, 1970).

Descartes, René, *Meditations on first philosophy*, trans. and ed. by John Cottingham (Cambridge, 1996).

Hume, David, *An Enquiry concerning the Principles of Morals*, ed. Tom Beauchamp (Oxford, 1998).

—*A Treatise of Human Nature*, ed. David and Mary Norton (Oxford, 2000).

—*An Enquiry concerning Human Understanding*, ed. Peter Millican (Oxford, 2007).

In the case of the works by Descartes and Hume, there are many other excellent editions available, including some good electronic versions.

# II Secondary reading

In offering this selection, I have tried to identify material that is, as far as possible, relatively easy to understand (much of it has been written with students or the general reader in mind), while yet either taking certain issues further than I have been able to in this short work or offering alternative interpretations to the ones that I have adopted. Many of the books listed below include extensive bibliographies.

## General

Collections:

*The Cambridge Companion to Kant and Modern Philosophy*, ed. Paul Guyer (Cambridge, 2006).

*The Cambridge Companion to Kant*, ed. Paul Guyer (Cambridge, 1992).

*A Companion to Kant*, ed. Graham Bird (Oxford, 2006).

*The Continuum Companion to Kant*, (eds) Gary Banham, Dennis Schulting and Nigel Hems (London, 2012).

Single works:

Paul Guyer, *Kant* (London, 2006).

Andrew Ward, *Kant: The Three Critiques* (Cambridge, 2006).

# Knowledge and metaphysics: *Critique of Pure Reason*

Collections:
*The Cambridge Companion to Kant's Critique of Pure Reason*, ed. Paul Guyer (New York, 2010).
*Kant's Critique of Pure Reason: Critical Essays*, ed. Patricia Kitcher (Lanham, 1998).

Single works:
Allison, Henry E., *Kant's Transcendental Idealism: An Interpretation and Defense* (New Haven, CT, rev. edn, 2004).
Dicker, Georges, *Kant's Theory of Knowledge: An Analytical Introduction* (Oxford, 2004).
Gardner, Sebastian, *Kant and the Critique of Pure Reason* (London, 1999).
Lovejoy, Arthur O., 'On Kant's Reply to Hume' in Molke Gram ed. *Kant: Disputed Questions* (Chicago, 1967).
Quinton, Anthony, 'Spaces and Times' *Philosophy* 37 (1962).
Savile, Anthony, *Kant's Critique of Pure Reason: An Orientation to the Central Theme* (Oxford, 2005).
Strawson, P. F., *The Bounds of Sense* (London, 1966).
—'Kant on Substance', *Entity and Identity and Other Essays* (Oxford, 1997).
Stroud, Barry, 'Transcendental Arguments' and 'The Allure of Idealism', *Understanding Human Knowledge* (Oxford, 2000).

# Morality: *Groundwork, Critique of Practical Reason* and *The Metaphysics of Morals*

Collection:
*Kant's Groundwork of the Metaphysics of Morals: Critical Essays*, ed. Paul Guyer (Lanham, 1998).

Single works:
Aune, Bruce, *Kant's Theory of Morals* (Princeton, 1979).
Beck, Lewis W., *A Commentary on Kant's Critique of Practical Reason* (Chicago, 1960).
Herman, Barbara, *The Practice of Moral Judgment* (Cambridge, MA, 1993).
Hill, Thomas E., Jr, *Dignity and Practical Reason in Kant's Moral Theory* (Ithaca, NY, 1992).

Korsgaard, Christine M., *Creating the Kingdom of Ends* (Cambridge, 1996).

Moore, A. W., *Noble in Reason, Infinite in Faculty: Themes and Variations in Kant's Moral and Political Philosophy* (London, 2003).

O'Neill, Onora, *Acting on Principle: An Essay on Kantian Ethics* (New York, 1975).

—*Constructions of Reason: Explorations of Kant's Practical Philosophy* (Cambridge, 1990).

Paton, H. J., *The Categorical Imperative: A Study in Kant's Moral Philosophy* (London, 1947).

Rawls, John, 'Themes in Kant's Moral Philosophy', in E. Forster ed., *Kant's Transcendental Deductions* (Stanford, CA, 1989).

— 'Kant' in *Lectures in the History of Moral Philosophy* (Cambridge, MA, 2000).

Reath, Andrews, 'Two Conceptions of the Highest Good in Kant', *Journal of the History of Philosophy* 26 (1988).

Silber, John, 'Kant's Conception of the Highest Good as Immanent and Transcendent', *Philosophical Review* 68 (1959).

Sullivan, Roger J., *An Introduction to Kant's Ethics* (Cambridge, 1994).

Timmermann, Jens, *Kant's Groundwork of the Metaphysics of Morals: A Commentary* (Cambridge, 2007).

N.B. the translations of the *Groundwork* by Beck, Paton and Zweig (listed above) also contain detailed analyses or critical essays on that work.

# INDEX